"Gea Gort and Mats Tunehag have gathered some of the best, experienced leaders to deal with this topic in clarity, using inspiring and challenging stories. Sadly, Business as Mission is not yet much on the agenda of Christians and churches. May this book reverse this and the kingdom of God be advanced. I pray that many Christians will see themselves as missionaries in business, leading a new generation to impact the world."

—Evi Rodemann, Chair
YLGen Connect Groups, Lausanne International

"In *BAM Global Movements*, Gea Gort and Mats Tunehag provide an excellent introduction to Business as Mission (BAM). The authors lay a solid foundation for BAM from a biblical and historical perspective, and on this foundation they address a wide variety of topics facing BAM entrepreneurs. The biggest contribution of the book, however, is the rich insight gleaned from the stories of real-life BAM entrepreneurs. Each chapter includes stories from the field of practitioners facing challenges of operating in corrupt, less-developed countries, addressing human trafficking, generating a multidimensional return on investment, and more. Tunehag's experience within the BAM ecosystem lends credibility to the book and allows for connections with BAM practitioners from around the world."

—Dr. Ross O'Brien, Director
The Center for Business as Mission, Dallas Baptist University

"BAM has become a movement to redefine 'mission,' 'missionary,' and 'mission field' in the twenty-first century. The church has to influence specific groups of business entrepreneurs by placing missional entrepreneurs as the new mission model. It will take path-breaking thoughts in creating wealth, especially the Global South entrepreneurs, to bring the gospel across the world. The BAM movement will create new thinking in mission models, and Global South entrepreneurs will sustain themselves, reducing the dependency factors in the future. I personally dialogued on many occasions with Mats Tunehag, who has pioneered and led the BAM movement. Therefore, I wholeheartedly endorse this book as both authors explain the way forward in creative ways of spreading the gospel across the world."

—Dr. K. Rajendran, Chair
Global Innovative Voices & Associates, GIVA Inno-Ventures
Former Chair, World Evangelical Alliance Mission Commission

"In *BAM Global Movement*, the authors demonstrate ingenuity and creativity in action through intriguing stories of good-news entrepreneurs who are making history with Jesus. Through these stories, we see how people around the world are following David Livingstone's admonition: that the good news of the gospel must be accompanied by economic development. For without economic development, there will be a significant lack in sustainable development from our mission efforts."

—Don Stephens, Founder/President
Mercy Ships, Lindale, Texas

"Thankfully, there are now many authors who have written on the theology of business and its importance in God's kingdom. However, the variety of examples and stories in this book truly bring it to life in a way that is clear and compelling. It is time that God's purpose for business becomes a global movement!"

—Bonnie P. Wurzbacher
Former Senior Vice President, The Coca-Cola Company
Chief Resource Development Officer, World Vision International

"BAM Global Movement is BAM at its best, TED-Talk style. Topics are discussed briefly and then followed by practical cases studies that most any church or organization can identify with. The book is full of case studies from around the globe, showcasing money-making, life-impacting business owners. These stories show that there is not only one way of doing BAM or running one kind of BAM business. If you read the book just for the case studies, it would be worth the price. Every Christian who has a job should be working for God first and foremost for the glory of Jesus. Not their boss, not for a paycheck. If anyone still questions the importance of Business as Mission in reaching the world and value of integrating faith and work, read this book!"

—Patrick Lai, OPEN Network

"According to 2 Corinthians 5, Christians are ambassadors of Christ in reconciling the world to God, and Business as Mission is an effective way to achieve this mandate. No wonder it has developed into a global movement. This book shows both BAM concepts and practical stories that exhibit the reality of the movement. This book is a must-read for any Christian who desires to learn more about BAM."

—Jeffrey J. Lee, Founder and Global CEO, SfK Ministries

"As a university-level teacher, I welcome this new collection of essays on BAM. I happen to believe that the Great Commission of Matthew 28 is nonexclusive in the sense that all human institutions—including business and all people, including entrepreneurs—are called by God to make disciples. BAM offers unique opportunities for entrepreneurs to engage in the Great Commission while outworking their vocational calling. This book will inspire and equip. I will be using it as a reference for my students. It will nicely complement the small literature on BAM that emerged about a decade ago."

—Dr. Rod St Hill, Vice President, Academic
Christian Heritage College, Brisbane, Australia

"I am so encouraged that this book has been written by two great writers. It is of utmost importance to have Mats' explanation and overview of this 'crazy thing' called 'Business as Mission.' I love Gea's foundational content and her efforts to help us overcome the stumbling blocks to understand and engage with BAM. And, of course, I love the diversity of the stories told of Business as Mission in action; I have engaged with many of them personally over the years. I have been waiting for a BAM book to recommend to our audience, and this is the one."

—Mark Plummer, Director, Business as Mission Resource Team

"Connecting business broadly defined to Christianity and faith has made enormous progress in recent decades. Gea Gort and Mats Tunehag add to that progress through this book. This work is full of individuals and teams putting into practice principles that demonstrate God's intention for work, life, and wealth. Readers of this book will better understand how God is at work through his people in all walks of life."

—Bob Doll, Chief Equity Strategist, Nuveen Asset Management

"This book is authentic and useful. Everywhere I go, I get questions about the meaning and examples of BAM. I thank Gea and Mats. This book is my answer."

—Dong Ho Song, General Secretary, International BAM Alliance

"So often misrepresented as an entry platform for ill-equipped missionaries, Business as Mission is revealed here in powerful and provocative narrative as simply the missional discipleship of God's people—entrepreneurs, business owners, managers—all shaped in the image of our eternally creative God."

—Mark Oxbrow, International Director, Faith2Share

BAM GL⚲BAL MOVEMENT

GEA GORT & MATS TUNEHAG

BAM GL⊕BAL MOVEMENT

business as mission
CONCEPTS & STORIES

BAM Global Movement: Business as Mission Concept and Stories

© 2018 Gea Gort and Mats Tunehag
Hendrickson Publishers Marketing, LLC
P. O. Box 3473
Peabody, Massachusetts 01961-3473
www.hendrickson.com

ISBN 978-1-68307-087-0

Unless otherwise noted, the Scripture quotations contained herein are taken from the Holy Bible, New International Version˚, NIV˚. Copyright © 1973, 1978, 1984, 2011 by Biblica, Inc.™ Used by permission of Zondervan. All rights reserved worldwide. www.zondervan.com. The "NIV" and "New International Version" are trademarks registered in the United States Patent and Trademark Office by Biblica, Inc.™

Unless otherwise indicated, all photographs were taken by Gea Gort and used here by permission.

Printed in the United States of America

First Printing — April 2018

Jacket and case cover design by Karol Bailey

This book has been made possible thanks to the support and funding of the Global Council of the International Foursquare Church.

CONTENTS

APPENDICES

FOREWORD

In 2006, I was part of a group that went to the Central African Republic to help a small NGO assess the viability of starting a microfinance program there. We quickly learned that there was a deeper, more challenging issue than starting a microfinance program. Although the country has a high percentage of Christians, too many of them have isolated the gospel from daily life. Their gospel was about going to heaven when they died, but it had nothing to say to the corruption, poverty, AIDS, or lack of opportunity in their country. On the other hand, starting a business, even a microbusiness, was challenging because of corruption, the wrong attitude of many in the church, and the lack of any supportive infrastructure (enforcement of contracts, transportation, banking, education, or healthcare).

This realization took us back to the basics in our thinking about doing "Business as Mission." What do we really mean by "business," and how is business connected with the gospel? And what do we really mean by "mission," and how is mission related to starting a business? Understanding Business as Mission (BAM) ultimately depends on how we define business and how we define our mission.

Business and the Kingdom of God

The tide is turning, but there is still a view of business, held by Christians and by society in general, that focuses on making money. To paraphrase Milton Friedman, the Nobel Prize-winning economist, business is about making as much money as you can within the constraints of the law. This singular focus has pushed many businesses to the edge (Enron and Volkswagen are poster cases for where this can lead), and certainly to a negative place in public perception. The statement "It's not personal, it's just business" conveys this view.

We mustn't take this view of business into BAM. It is issues like these that ignited a search for a more biblical view of mission and business. Scripture has a great deal to say about the importance of our daily work, and also about the role of the institution of business. For the past ten years, I have been a part of the Theology of Work Project (www.theologyofwork.org), and we have written a commentary on every book of the Bible and what each has to say about daily work.

To understand business, we need to start with a biblical view of work. Beginning in Genesis, we see that God himself is a worker. The Bible does not open with the statement, "In the beginning, God preached a sermon." Throughout the rest of Scripture, we see instructions, guidance, and illustrations of how we are to do our work to the glory of God. As Paul instructed the Colossians, "Whatever you do, work at it with all your heart as working for the Lord and not for man. . . . It is the Lord Christ you are serving."

Business

As we see in the Scriptures, when people moved from living off the land to living in a city, they moved from self-sufficiency to interdependence. It is business that provides the goods and services needed for life in this world. Business, as an institution in society, is fundamental for the flourishing of society that God speaks to, for example, in Jeremiah 29. In our present world, business provides the goods and services needed to enable communities to flourish, and the opportunity for people to work.

Business is the only institution that creates economic growth, and it is the source of funding for all other institutions. In other words, a real business makes a profit. As Mats Tunehag reminds us in chapter 11, "Business shall serve people, align with God's purposes, be good stewards of creation, and make a profit." While profit is necessary, however, it is not the real reason for business. In my interview with business leader Don Flow (*Ethix*, March 2004), he put it this way: "I don't know a healthy person who gets up in the morning and looks in the mirror and says I live for my blood. But

I don't know a person alive who doesn't have blood. Blood is like profit—necessary to live, but not the reason for living."

Indeed, the role of business in society goes far beyond profit, as the Wealth Creation Manifesto (see Appendix 1) states:

> Business has a special capacity to create financial wealth, but also has the potential to create different kinds of wealth for many stakeholders, including social, intellectual, physical and spiritual wealth. . . . Good business has intrinsic value as a means of material provision and can be an agent of positive transformation in society.

Scripture also has a great deal to say about how to run a business. For example, in Isaiah 58, we see that God doesn't hear the worship of his people when they mistreat their workers (58:3). Acting rightly in transactions is also a vital issue to God. "A false balance is an abomination to the LORD, but a just weight is his delight" (Prov. 11:1). Dishonest dealings are abhorrent to God, but honest dealings delight him!

But how do we navigate doing business the "right way" in many countries that suffer from corruption? This will never be easy. I remember being confronted with this issue when talking about business to the glory of God in Nepal. They challenged me with the context of their business dealings within an environment of bribery. When they asked me how they should handle their particular situation, I gave the question back to them because they knew the context of the work there much better than I. Corruption will always be a problem for doing business rightly, but there is also a difference between bribery and extortion. I asked them if they ever gathered to pray about how God could use them in the short term (making a difficult choice for a particular situation) and in the long term (being salt and light in their world to remove this accepted practice). They said this was an issue they rarely talked about because it was such a dirty and difficult subject. But I reminded them that God cares about these issues, and I urged them to pray together.

Some argue that these difficult situations mean that we cannot set up a legitimate business to God's glory in some places. Again, when we read the Scripture, we see that the world was no different in Jesus' time. His guidance in living out the kingdom, even in the middle of brokenness, is clear and important today. In *Bribery and Corruption: Biblical Reflections and Case Studies for the Marketplace in Asia*, Hwa Yung shows us how and why we should work incarnationally in the midst of broken circumstances. To dismiss business as a means only to another end misses something fundamental in Scripture and in our Christian faith. We cannot ignore the challenges of doing business to the glory of God, but we also cannot use these challenges as an excuse to not represent Christ where he has placed us.

Missions

Getting business right is essential to getting BAM right, but we also need to understand our mission. In chapter 1 of this book, Gea Gort asks and answers the powerful question: Have we shrunk the gospel? Mission fundamentally depends on how we define the gospel and how we understand God's redemptive plan. We often speak of the Great Commission (Matt. 28:18–20 ESV) when talking about the role of missions in spreading the gospel:

> And Jesus came and said to them, "All authority in heaven and on earth has been given to me. Go therefore and make disciples of all nations, baptizing them in the name of the Father and of the Son and of the Holy Spirit, teaching them to observe all that I have commanded you."

It is clear that he is commanding them to preach the good news of salvation leading to baptism. But it is equally clear that mission is bigger than this: "To make disciples . . . teaching them to observe all that I have commanded you." The truth about work and business is a part of the teaching of Christ, and it is also a part of what it means to make disciples. We must be careful about "shrinking the gospel."

This book expands our understanding of both business and mission. In chapter 9, Tunehag clearly outlines the three biblical mandates that are part of this mission: to be creative and good stewards in business (Creation Mandate) and serve our neighbors—that is, the various stakeholders in business (Great Commandment Mandate). But we should also do business as the Great Commission Mandate, and thus glorify God among all peoples. Then, in chapters 11 and 12, we learn about doing business as justice, business as creation care, business as loving your neighbor, and doing business as it relates to other biblical themes and values.

In Luke 4:18–19 (ESV), Jesus explained his own mission, quoting from Isaiah:

"The Spirit of the Lord is upon me,
      because he has anointed me
      to proclaim good news to the poor.
He has sent me to proclaim liberty to the captives
      and recovering of sight to the blind,
      to set at liberty those who are oppressed,
to proclaim the year of the Lord's favor."

Note his clear reference to poverty, brokenness, and freedom. As we see from Jesus, addressing these things is also a part of the gospel and needs to be a part of our mission.

As I was speaking on this topic to a group of pastors in the Central African Republic, one of the pastors stood up at the end and said, "I get what you are saying, but what is more important? To teach people about whole life discipleship as you have been speaking, or to teach people to believe in Jesus so they go to heaven when they die?" I told him that I used to work at a company where they make airplanes and that his question was like asking which wing of the airplane was more important for flight, the left wing or the right wing? Scripture teaches us that both are important, so we need to hold to that.

Business as Mission

For thirty-two years, I worked at The Boeing Company. Partway through my time there, I realized that I was in full-time Christian service, that my work mattered. It was often difficult, both because I live in a broken world and because I was also broken. But still, I realized that my work had meaning and purpose.

If we believe that God cares about what we do every day, and if we believe that God has placed us in our particular circumstances, then we need to put into practice what it means to do Business as Mission right where we are. We need to treat our work, particularly our work in business, as something sacred. Business as Mission is vital to God's purposes. It is about proclaiming and demonstrating the kingdom of God in the marketplace in all nations. We can do that through Business as Mission.

This Book

A natural question coming out of this discussion of Business as Mission asks: What does it really look like? You may say that you get the idea, but you're not really sure how it works.

BAM Global Movement makes a significant contribution to our understanding of Business as Mission. Besides explaining the concept, Gea Gort and Mats Tunehag offer fascinating case studies. We get to meet people around the world, see what they are doing, and understand how and why they did what they did and do what they do. With each concept chapter and portrait, the authors add details to our understanding of what it means to really do Business as Mission in a holistic way to the glory of God. They frame many questions about BAM through thinking about the various issues, and then they offer illustrations of how this is being done.

Whether you are considering embarking on a BAM venture yourself or simply want to understand BAM better, this is a vital resource. Thanks to Gea Gort and Mats Tunehag and to all the many people they introduce us to. God bless you.

Albert M. Erisman
Seattle, Washington

PREFACE

In the past two decades, there has been an unprecedented move to develop the Business as Mission (BAM) concept by examining the Holy Scriptures and learning from history, as well as from present-day BAM initiatives. There is a growing and God-inspired conceptual cohesion with regard to Business as Mission. There are also an increasing number of BAM business as well as networks on various levels. We can indeed speak of a growing global BAM movement.

Global Movement

The Business as Mission movement is a part of a broader global movement, as there are paradigm shifts taking place in the areas of mission, work, and aid. It's about (re)discovering the scope of the gospel, the meaning of work, and the value of business. It's about seeking business solutions to global issues, while embracing community and the value of the local place in a global world.

In part one of this book, Gea Gort provides insight as to how these shifts "feed" the global BAM movement, reflecting on BAM from a church and mission perspective. The stories in this section demonstrate these perspectives through interviews with church and mission leaders, aid workers, and academics on a journey of implementing BAM.

Concept

Business as Mission has roots and a history. Its roots are in who God is and who we are—humans created in his image. BAM is not new. People throughout history have tried to align their lives and business with God's purposes and biblical values. BAM is about shaping business for God and for the common good, having a positive impact on multiple bottom lines for multiple stakeholders.

In part two, Mats Tunehag will explain the BAM concept—about the theology of work and business, as well as biblical views of profit and holistic transformation through business. He also explores BAM from historical and global perspectives, as well as paints some future scenarios.

Stories

Each concept chapter alternates with interviews with BAM practitioners from around the globe. The thirty stories in this book show that there is not just one way of doing BAM or running one kind of BAM business, nor is BAM limited to one particular industry, nor can BAM be claimed by any one church denomination. Rather, these stories indicate that thousands of Christians around the globe are proactively trying to connect their Sunday beliefs with Monday praxis.

In the final chapters, Mats provides further insights into the present global BAM movement. To strengthen BAM and move it forward, all parts of the body of Christ are needed, as in an ecosystem. It is encouraging to see church denominations, mission organizations, seminaries, and business schools starting to discover and embrace BAM.

Both of us believe that BAM can and should be an integral part of business solutions to local challenges, as well as global issues in today's highly urbanized world. Although these brief concept chapters and stories do not claim to be an exhaustive depiction of BAM, we hope they will serve as a helpful introduction to this important movement.

Gea Gort, The Netherlands
Mats Tunehag, Sweden

Acknowledgments

A book is bigger than its author. There are many people and circumstances that shape every author and thus each book. These are always too many to mention, but I want to acknowledge my family, friends, colleagues and supporters, who have all been a part of this journey. I will venture to mention three specifically.

First, my wonderful wife, who is a source of joy and encouragement. We have endless conversations about all manner of things, including the issues dealt with in this book.

Second, my closest BAM colleague over the years, Jo Plummer. Our collaboration through BAM Global Think Tank and beyond informed these chapters and also provided connections to many of the people who tell their stories in this book.

Last but not least, a special thank you to Lane Proctor for spending countless hours editing my chapters for clarity and checking grammar and spelling! Thanks also for all of your valuable comments and suggestions.

Mats Tunehag

As Mats rightly pointed out, "A book is bigger than its author." Many have invested in my life, but I want to particularly mention Menno, my beloved partner in life whose support sustains me and keeps me happy and smiling! I also want to acknowledge the investment of my BGU family. This innovative university expanded my horizon through their way of teaching—academic and practical—while connecting me with amazing people around the globe.

Regarding the whole BAM endeavor, I would like to mention especially Monique and Tiemen Fahner, whose involvement and advice have been so valuable, and the Global Council of Foursquare, whose financial support enabled me to collect the many stories in this book.

Mats and I also want to express our gratitude to Patricia Anders for her patience and helpful editing work. We also want to extend thanks to Al Erisman for the foreword and for recommending this book idea to publisher Paul Hendrickson.

Gea Gort

PART I

BAM in Light of a Broader Movement

By Gea Gort

INTRODUCTION

By Gea Gort

In the following concept parts, I will explain how Business as Mission is an expression of a much broader movement, a movement happening all over the globe with different aspects. In broad strokes, I will paint a bigger picture with the aim of providing general oversight and insight into theological concepts and ideas that are shifting. I agree with what a friend of mine recently said: "Five hundred years ago we had a Reformation of dogma. Now we have a reformation of mission."

What does this reformation look like? In one sentence, it is a missional way of living out the *whole incarnated gospel* in our daily life, where we work and where we live. While this may sound good and sensible, some (sub)conscious beliefs could be hindering us in doing so. Therefore, before Mats zooms into the concept of Business as Mission, let's first consider how we view mission, work, aid, place, and community.

The stories in this first part show that Business as Mission is not just a "business thing." All over the globe and in diverse ways, mission and aid agencies—as well as church leaders, planters, and pioneers—are engaging in BAM. The final story of this section shows how an international church denomination is incorporating BAM into their circle and Bible college.

But first, let's consider the story of my friend, Faouzi Chihabi. This Dutchman of Moroccan descent has made a remarkable journey: he studied theology, was a pastor, and is now owner of a top-end restaurant. In this journey, Faouzi gained some interesting insights along the way.

Moroccan Faouzi Chihabi (The Netherlands)

A Restaurant with a Mission

Faouzi Chihabi(left) with coworkers Carlos
Andrade Vezo and Francis Liz Barnier.

"Through working in my business, I'm experiencing more of God," says Faouzi Chihabi. "I have my faith in my head and heart, but now it's also flowing through my hands." Faouzi studied theology to become a minister, and then worked on issues concerning vulnerable youth for both the Dutch and European governments. Presently, he owns the trattoria Borgo d'Aneto. On the riverside in Rotterdam, his former work experience and his faith merge in this restaurant-with-a-mission.

The latte macchiato is poured carefully. The Italian bun is crisp; not too soft and not too hard. The plate nicely decorated with fresh vegetables. Faouzi trains his crew to keep an eye on the customer. In every area of this restaurant, they pursue a high-quality standard.

Borgo d'Aneto (www.borgodaneto.nl) is an approved apprenticeship for youth "at risk" who attend special schools offering vocational training. Faouzi reacts strongly to the assumption that it is an extra challenge to maintain high quality with these young people working in his restaurant. "These boys and girls might have a low IQ, but it's the biggest misconception that they are not socially adept. They are actually very sensitive and intuitive." He sees them flourish in his restaurant, although sometimes a meal ends up in the trash. "As a business we cannot afford to put something on the table that doesn't meet a good standard. When a plate is thrown in the trash, these youngsters might feel they themselves landed there, but they learn through failure to continue, despite a setback. They realize their contribution matters, and that realization causes growth."

The Remedial Effects of "Real Work"

Faouzi knows the ins and outs of working with vulnerable youth. Before he became a restaurant owner, he worked in this field for the municipal government at district level. He later became involved in research at the European level, where he developed an educational program that involved simulating businesses so youth could experience the "real world" in a classroom setting. He realized, however, that this wasn't the same as working in an actual business. "I have to address these young people if they are doing it wrong, because the survival of my business depends on how they perform. A teacher in a simulated business setting can permit them to shy away from confrontation. Creating such a 'safe learning environment' is unhealthy for other reasons. Young people can become frightened with warnings like 'here it is safe, but later in the real world . . . !' Youth need to learn that failure is a part of life."

"Youth need to learn that failure is a part of life."

Background

Faouzi can identify himself with these "problem youth." He was born in Morocco and came as a child to Antwerp in Belgium, where he grew up in a difficult family situation. Around the age of twenty, his curiosity was stirred by a friend of African descent, who changed in a positive way after his conversion to Christianity. "I started reading the Bible," recalls Faouzi. "The Sermon on the Mount especially impressed me, which is full of examples of how God cares for us as a Father. I came to believe it was true. As a Muslim I was used to understanding truth rationally, but this became a deep soul issue. It was an irresistible and beautiful inner feeling, which I couldn't resist. I prayed the sinner's prayer on my own and God's Spirit came over me. It felt like a shower, an overwhelming inner cleansing."

He studied theology, but during his first year as an apprentice in a little town, he saw too little of a connection between the pastor and the regular, daily life of the congregation. "It felt oppressive to me. Too often the life of a pastor revolves around sermons, management, and pastoral work. I saw a danger of living in an ivory tower, far away from the reality of life. What intrigued me was how a pastor could understand the daily problems people face in their work and family."

Connecting Theory and Practice

Distance between theory and practice is not only a problem in the church but also in wider society. According to Faouzi, "In our schools we teach mainly theory. It's like we teach the 'definition of walking,' but we learn to walk by falling down! A few centuries ago, education was for the elite. Now education has become 'a must' for everyone. But entire groups of young people feel imprisoned in our educational institutions, where the emphasis is on learning by using your head, with hardly any appreciation for working with heart and hands."

He firmly believes that the normal working life should be much closer to young people. "Government legislation in most Western countries contributes to a dualistic way of thinking. A ten-year-old boy comes here regularly. He wants to do something, but I cannot give him a few euros to bring empty bottles away, because that could be considered here in the Netherlands as child labor and get me into trouble as a business owner. But this boy's confidence could grow if I commend him on a job well done. Instead of stimulating his work ethic, our society chooses to postpone his work identity to a later time. He is forced to get bored and hang out on the street. Is that what we want?"

Don't think in boxes—saturate the entire company with humanity.

According to Faouzi, this thinking-in-boxes is undermining society, and he sees it everywhere. "When I meet management leaders of large companies to talk with them about corporate social responsibility, they tell me: 'Social responsibility? Go to that office, that department is taking care of it. Another company sponsors African children and has pictures of them on the wall. Wonderful, right? But are we then turning away to continue our focus solely on business profits? The question is how we integrate humanity and make that part of the DNA of the entire business, including management and products." For Faouzi "doing good" isn't some kind of tithe to God and society; he wants to saturate the entire company with humanity. Faith and God are central in that aim.

Host and Fatherhood

"God is a generous God. He is a God of abundance," continues Faouzi. "He is the ultimate host. How can we reflect that in our restaurant?" God as Father is another source of inspiration for Faouzi. A father is someone who stands next to you; approachable, accessible, and close. "At first I was not planning to run this restaurant or work in the kitchen myself, but the managers and chefs I hired did not want to work with the youth the way I had in mind. Cleaning toilets? They objected to cleaning toilets, that was a job for trainees! In my opinion, a leader works alongside his people and rolls up his sleeves as well."

"When I am busy with creating . . . God is unfolding himself."

Not only is business holy, but all work is holy. "It is not a coincidence that the first verse in the Bible begins with God creating heaven and earth. The first time God's name is mentioned, it is connected to work: God created. I myself did all the spiritual exercises that you can imagine. I have prayed and fasted, because I desired to know what God wants, but every time there seemed to be some kind of distance. Please allow me to speak from my own experience, but I've never experienced God's presence before as I do now. When I am busy with creating here in this restaurant, God is unfolding himself."

A Big Dream

Faouzi has found a way to connect work, life experiences, and faith. Meanwhile, he continues to work side by side with vulnerable young people, interacting together with clients from different backgrounds. He finds ways to make God's heart tangible on the work floor: as a father of young people, as a host for his guests, as a creator of concrete products. But this is not "mission accomplished." On the contrary, Faouzi feels the need to bring appreciation for craftsmanship back into society and wants more people and businesses to get involved in transferring craftsman skills to young people. In his own neighborhood, he would love to see more of that kind of business activity. Although his restaurant is fully booked most of the time, this is not his measure of success. His dreams are bigger.

CHAPTER 1

DID WE SHRINK
THE GOSPEL?

Rediscovering the Scope of God's Mission

By Gea Gort

Christians have different views and priorities when it comes to mission. Depending on tradition and personality, some focus on witness and prayer to bring people to eternal salvation, while others emphasize the importance of good deeds and are involved in social projects, especially to help the marginalized. Whatever the focus and interest, these aspects are indeed all part of mission, as well as being a witness through our changed and loving lives as followers of Christ.

The aspects described above had been my general understanding of mission, since I worked for many years as a missionary on board Mercy Ships' hospital ships. Its crew came from over forty nations and many more denominations. Living and working together with people of such diverse backgrounds broadened my views, but while studying with Bakke Graduate University (BGU) my assumptions as an evangelical were stretched again. I had an "aha" moment when reading a discussion between Eastern Orthodox and evangelical theologians. "We agree about the core of Christ's redemptive work," explained the Eastern Orthodox. "But there is more than the core; evangelicals tend to shrink the gospel. There is much more to it!"[1] This discussion fueled my search into what this "more" could be.

---

1. *Three Views on Eastern Orthodox Evangelicalism*, ed. James J. Stamoolis (Grand Rapids: Zondervan, 2004). Contributor Bradley Nassif's main argument is that "evangelicalism" is also at the core of Orthodoxy (authority of the Bible, Trinity, Christ centeredness, etc.), and refers to the "minimalism" of the evangelicals: "The

A Missional God

For many decades, mission was mainly linked to Jesus' commandment, "Therefore go and make disciples of all nations" (Matt. 28:19), which became known as the "Great Commission" under the influence of William Carey—at least within a large part of the Protestant world, as he was one of the first overseas missionaries in the eighteenth century.

According to British missiologist Chris Wright, however, mission is much more than sending out a few missionaries, organizing an evangelistic event, or running a social project. In his book *The Mission of God*,[2] he argues that the entire Bible both directly and indirectly is about the story of God and his mission. Since mission is part of who God is, mission belongs to him. Mission is not our project, something we do, or a few people we send out. Instead, it is part of the DNA of every Christian since his Spirit dwells within us. God desires to show redemption through our lives, while expressing it in all facets of life on earth.

Living out God's Story

We are invited on the stage to act out God's mission in our day and time. This is another way to imagine a missional life, which is suggested by Anglican theologian N. T. Wright. He invites us to discover the redemptive storyline in the Bible, study its characters, and go "on stage." It's our turn to act out "the Story" (simplified in my words).[3] Wright also argues that when we consider Jesus' words and deeds in the context of the Jewish culture of his time, these words and deeds have much more implications for our life on earth than

---

inner-circle includes doctrines that both groups hold as essential; the larger outer circle includes doctrines the Orthodox hold to be essential, but evangelicals generally do not" (84). With the outer circle, Nassif means the Orthodox incarnational Trinitarian vision of life (more holistic versus dualism and a positive view of creation, "the Word became flesh") and their value of corporate communion (versus individualism).

2. Christopher J. H. Wright, *The Mission of God: Unlocking the Bible's Grand Narrative* (Downers Grove, IL: IVP Academic, 2006).

3. N. T. Wright, "How Can the Bible Be Authoritative?"; see esp. "The Authority of a Story," http://ntwrightpage.com/2016/07/12/how-can-the-bible-be-authoritative/.

we have assumed for a long time.[4] It's not only about salvation but also about bringing God's *shalom* into the spheres of life in which we are involved.

Mission out of Overflow

Jesus talked often about his kingdom being near, and he prayed in the Lord's Prayer, "Your kingdom come, your will be done, on earth as it is in heaven." Finding that kingdom is like finding a pearl of great value (Matt. 13:46). We received this pearl free of charge, which enriches our lives in so many ways. Out of this overflow, we desire to share that wealth. That desire is mission. The kingdom is about justice, love, and righteousness. It is about redemption and restoring *all* things to God. It is about God's love impacting and changing the way we view ourselves and our relationships, communities, structures, and world.

Living in the "In-between Time"

When we get a taste of true life, we sense that there is an enormous source of transforming power available. At the same time, we live among brokenness and see only glimpses of his kingdom. We live in an "in-between time": Jesus went back to heaven, left the Holy Spirit to do greater works than he had done, and promised that all things will be made new when he returns. Theologians call this time the "now and not yet." Meanwhile, God challenges us to seek his kingdom and promises us that when we seek, we will find. But it's not all straightforward; it's a search, a journey. God gave us his word, but the Bible is not a clear guidance book, like some sort of dishwasher manual. Instead he gave humans brains, emotions, and free will, and we are challenged to seek how his principles apply in our day and time. This allows for different expressions within the diverse contexts of place and time: humans shaping the world in cooperation with him, because of a heart connection with the Creator. Discovering these implications, however, is a lifelong journey. It's as if we look through stained glass windows and realize that much is a mystery to us.

---

4. N. T. Wright, *The Challenge of Jesus* (Downers Grove, IL: InterVarsity Press, 1999).

Summary

Business as Mission is an expression of a reawakening that mission encompasses much more than eternity, a good moral life, or good works. BAM entrepreneurs realize that mission isn't restricted to a few Christian professionals, such as pastors or missionaries. God is on a mission, and all of us are participants living out the Story of God's mission. BAM entrepreneurs are on a journey, seeking to find out how this can look in their contexts. They want to live out this transforming power on earth. They don't want to leave this power in storage and wait to see its effects in a far future; they want to express God's kingdom now within the broken systems of our day—with hope, faith, and love. They have hope for a complete restoration at the return of Jesus, but they also believe that God can do much more than we pray and hope for.

Georges Dubi (Switzerland)

Mission Organization Develops Business to Rebuild Countries

Soon after the Berlin Wall fell, Georges Dubi saw the need to initiate, support, and encourage business in Eastern Europe. Swiss-based Christliche Ostmission gave him the opportunity to do so in Romania. Ever since, the mission has been involved in helping develop the business sector, also in other developing countries. "So much more is possible," says Georges, "If we are open to be inspired by God, learn to think beyond ourselves, and are willing to take risks."

Georges is someone who tends to see opportunities, evidenced by the fact that he started businesses while traveling in Morocco in his early twenties. Even though he was successful in Morocco, he felt God had another plan for his life. Georges had come to faith a year before in his home country of Switzerland after walking into a church coffee shop. Georges is a reflective person; he has a strong intuition and an antenna for the spiritual world. "When I walked into that coffee shop, I knew I had come home."

Back in Switzerland, Georges started working for Christliche Ostmission (www.ostmission.ch), one of the larger Swiss mission agencies, and helped with smuggling Bibles into Eastern Europe. While working in that part of the world, he again saw business opportunities and started selling navigation equipment to police departments. "This company provided a cover and lots of contacts; I knew people, which gave me also insight with who and where to be extra cautious."

After the Berlin Wall fell in 1989, Georges saw the need to develop the Eastern European business sector. "Shortly after the Wall fell, I went to Romania. At the border, I saw long lines of trucks with relief supplies. I knew: 'The Romanians shouldn't start depending on our aid, but get help to start businesses so they can stand on their own feet.'"

"[They] shouldn't start depending on our aid, but get help to start businesses so they can stand on their own feet."

The Supernatural

Like Georges "knew" he had come home when walking into the coffee shop as a teenager, similarly he "knew" what was expected of him this time. "We need to be open for the supernatural," is Georges' conviction. It happens to him regularly that he "just knows"; but instead of talking to colleagues and management about divine revelations, he presents a well thought-out plan. "If the plan is adopted, I see that as a confirmation that I heard right." So shortly after the wall fell, that is what he did. The plan was accepted by the management and board of Ostmission, and they gave him a budget of 150,000 Swiss francs. Although that was a rather large amount for the mission organization, it was just a drop in the bucket to stimulate the business sector in a country. "It started very, very small," recalls Georges. "We faced a huge challenge. During the communist era, Christians were being discriminated against; they were hardly trained and had poorly paid jobs. We had to start from scratch. So we developed business training, helped with finding quality, secondhand equipment, which they could buy and pay back because we gave them small loans."

A Brilliant Move

Meanwhile, the Swiss government realized the importance of developing the economic sector of their eastern neighbors and heard about Ostmission's endeavors. The mission presented a plan to the government but wondered if a secular government would fund a mission organization.

"They knew what we did and liked our plan," recalls Georges. Over a period of several years, the mission was able to obtain funding for millions, if they promised to not evangelize and would also make the training accessible for non-Christians. Ostmission wondered whether it was right to take the offer. Would they be denying their Christian mission? "At first we argued among our staff that we wouldn't have to take the limitations literally; after all, we had smuggled Bibles before, which had been illegal also. But that argument didn't feel right; we wanted to walk in integrity. After much discussion, we decided to accept the offer, keep to the rules, and see how things would work out."

It proved a brilliant move, because now they came—as Christians—into contact with whole other spheres in society. It is Georges' experience that business opens doors: "The business world is relational. We had many personal conversations with influential people and operated on an entirely different level." Meanwhile, they adapted the training, keeping to the content while rephrasing it. Non-Christians following the training program commented that they liked the "special atmosphere." A relationship with the Swiss government developed as well. They came to check Ostmission's activities regularly and liked what they saw. As a result, the mission was asked to explain the principles taught in more detail to the government, since the government wanted to introduce and implement these principles within the department in Switzerland. "It all worked out beyond our expectations," says Georges. "It was remarkable."

Meanwhile, a Romanian foundation, ROMCOM, was set up to stimulate business and became independent over time. Georges is still on their board and has since become the director of Ostmission in Switzerland. Stimulating entrepreneurship in developing countries has his keen interest. The experience gained in Romania is helping the mission to know how to stimulate development in other countries. Georges says, "Some entrepreneurs who have attended our courses in Romania in the beginning are now influential businesspeople. What started small has grown enormously. For example, a small Romanian garage owner was asked by a senior executive of Volkswagen to be their representative in Romania. The international board of VW had questions because he was such 'an insignificant owner of a small garage,' but he just radiated reliability and integrity. It turned out to be a good choice, because VW has been most successful in Romania of all Eastern European countries."

"So much more is possible."

Georges stresses the importance to be open to receive supernatural inspiration. "We tend to think too small," he says in a calm and gentle manner. "We limit ourselves to what we see and think in the natural. We need to think much bigger, because when we step out into the impossible we also become aware how much we need God. I learned that he desires to provide. So much more is possible."

Arleen Westerhof (The Netherlands)
"We Have a Mandate to Act"

Arleen Westerhof initiated the European Economic Summit. Since 2014, Christians active in the area of business, economics, and policymaking have gathered yearly in Amsterdam. Before starting the EES, Arleen prayed fervently for influential Christians to rise up. She now witnesses answers to these prayers: "I see skilled and anointed followers of Jesus Christ all around the globe involved in social transformational movements."

Arleen Westerhof is familiar with the corporate world. As a Canadian of Jamaican descent, she earned a doctorate in chemistry and moved to the Netherlands to work as expatriate at a multinational company. While in the Netherlands, she met and married Dick Westerhof. They both felt a call to start and pastor a charismatic church in Amsterdam: God's Embassy.

Dick has a professional job in addition to being a pastor, and over the years the Westerhofs' interest for business and economy didn't decrease while leading the church but rather increased. The financial crisis fueled this interest, and in 2013 Arleen began fervently praying that God would raise up current-day Daniels, Esthers, and Josephs, and that they would gain in wisdom and grow in stature. Toward the end of that year, Arleen couldn't shake off the urge to act and become part of the answer to her prayers herself.

European Economic Summit

"I started getting all kinds of ideas," shares Arleen. "Like the importance of bringing together economic thinkers and business practitioners. Business leaders do get microlevel education and support from their churches and Christian networks on how to be a good example, morally and ethically. That is important, but they also need macro insight on issues such as unethical structures. I also began to wonder what kind of Holy Spirit-inspired ideas were around. Who were the God-inspired economic thinkers and business owners? How did they translate biblical principles to contemporary issues? I wanted to create a place where those kinds of people could meet, fellowship, and exchange ideas." Arleen researched and then felt God's guidance as she got into contact with influential Christians on key positions, who knew that being called and anointed by God would make an impact in their sphere of influence. They encouraged Arleen to go ahead, and as a result the European Economic Summit (http://economicsummit.eu) was born.

Present-day Daniels, Esthers, and Josephs

One of those who have become closely involved is businessman Graham Power, who started the movement Unashamedly Ethical in Africa with the aim of combating corruption. Another is Lisette Malmberg, an Aruban businesswoman and pastor, who started a social movement in Aruba. Also Bruno Roche, a French chief economist at Mars Incorporated, a food manufacturer with over 40 billion in sales annually. Among other tasks, here Bruno is involved in developing new economic business models that have the potential to solve the youth unemployment problem in Europe and to alleviate poverty in developing nations.

Arleen says, "We must seek together how we translate ideas inspired by the Holy Spirit in the public arena of economy and business, so that we can influence public opinion, allowing people to become receptive to the gospel. Previously, in many churches it was common to deliver the message that Christians should stay away from money and mammon; but now I see people with consecrated hearts getting involved, speaking up, and gaining influence."

"We must seek together how we translate ideas inspired by the Holy Spirit in the public arena of economy and business."

Within their own church setting, Arleen and Dick also encourage their members to discover their vocation in society, while challenging them to be aware of the problems, needs, and injustice within their spheres of influence and seek God for how they can bring change. "We want to stir up the gift of prophecy, because Christians are called to bring God's solutions to some of the most pressing problems of our times. The prophetic gift helps us to hear God's voice and know what to do. One couple from the church had a desire to see African businesses become more effective in alleviating poverty and helping to transform lives. After praying, they discovered that a major problem is that African companies do not have adequate access to global trade markets, and they decided to start a trading company to increase their access."

"A paradigm shift is going on," Arleen continues. "We are at the beginning of a new movement, and we are seeing some forerunners. These people give hope as they share their stories and show how it works, enabling others to see and grasp it also. It may take a generation for it to become commonplace to think from a spiritual perspective about world problems, but it is beginning to break through."

In addition to their yearly gatherings in Amsterdam, the European Economic Summit is also developing a think tank and catalyzing social movements. Meanwhile, Arleen is starting to organize similar summits on other continents. "I did put my foot in the water, but don't yet have a complete blueprint of what it will lead to. But I'm convinced that God is calling us to alleviate suffering. Jesus tells us and has anointed us to lay hands on the sick, but we are also—as it were—anointed to lay hands on sick systems. God is able to give us revelation and creativity so that we can bring constructive solutions. To be able to do so, we must be socially engaged—like Daniel, Esther, and Joseph. It's time to think bigger and act with knowledge, discernment, and wisdom. We have a mandate to act. It is time to stand up."

CHAPTER 2

THE WAVES OF A THEOLOGY OF WORK MOVEMENT

Historical and Eternal Perspectives on Work

By Gea Gort

There is a growing understanding that we should apply the whole gospel in all areas of our lives, which includes our lives at work. God shows himself as a God who works. At the same time, we are not to be work-centered but Christ-centered—we don't live to work but work to live for a higher purpose. How to express this purpose is the search of many. We could talk of a global Theology of Work (TOW) movement, as many Christians are realizing that the body of Christ needs to be better equipped: for example, the Theology of Work Project, an electronic resource on what the Bible says about work,[1] or Bakke Graduate University teaching TOW to seminaries around the globe and enabling pastors to equip their church members.[2]

---

1. The Theology of Work Project began with a question: What does the Bible have to say about our daily work? After seven years of work by an international project team, drawing on theological resources from many seminaries, they produced a commentary on the whole Bible. This resource is available electronically at www.theologyofwork.org and as a complete set from Hendrickson Publishers. Translation in various languages is proceeding (source: Al Erisman).

2. Since 2008, Bakke Graduate University (www.bgu.edu) has helped facilitate and develop Theology of Work curriculum, with the support of Mustard Seed Foundation. In seventy-five countries, over fifty thousand students followed a TOW course, taught at seminaries or marketplace networks, while many more spinoffs resulted. "It's hard to calculate the amount of students, but I see TOW mushrooming all over the place," says Lowell Bakke (personal correspondence, March 2017).

Our theological views regarding work need reevaluation. As we discuss in our concept chapters in part two of this book, and as a reoccurring theme in this stories section, we have inherited a dualistic mind-set where we consider our Christian lives to be spiritual—that is, belonging mainly to a Sunday church life—and we hardly seek God as to how we could bring his redemption into the different areas of our day-to-day work. The tide is changing, however, and many books about faith in the marketplace have been published over the past decades, but it is generally quiet from the Sunday pulpit when it comes to the area of work. It is rare to find vision, prayer, or commissioning for the mission of businesspeople or of everyday workers within their various fields of influence.

Dualistic Inheritance

Why is this dualistic thinking so persistent? Greek dualistic thinking has had its influence, where the spirit and intellect were considered worthwhile and secular, while mundane work was looked down upon and left to slaves. Salvation in Greek thinking is about the spirit, while in Hebrew (biblical) thinking a person is one: spirit, soul, and body. "Peace" from a Greek mind-set is about escaping the pressures of life. "Peace" in Hebrew thought is to actively take part in the *completion* of what is good and righteous.

Dualistic thinking has had its influence within Christianity, although we can find biblical teaching on the value of work within church history. For example, the idea of *Ora et Labora* (pray and labor) in Benedictine monasteries considers that through the mopping of floors, Christ is honored, the community served, and Christian character built. The Reformation also lifted the ordinary believing worker through their focus on "the priesthood of all believers." Luther famously said that the milkmaid was just as important as the church leaders drinking the milk at the table.

But in our minds, the monks mopped the floors of "holy" buildings, while priesthood is mostly restricted to "spiritual matters." As a result professionals, artists, technicians, economists, and businesspeople feel mundane and poorly equipped to exercise "priesthood" within their spheres of influence.

Our View of the End Times

There are different reasons why a dualistic mind-set can be so persistent. One of them is our idea concerning the "end times." Will only what is "spiritual" last, or will our daily work also have eternal value? Our beliefs about the future impact what we do today. When we expect that God will destroy the earth and all material things with it, why then bother with those material things? But when we believe that God will transform the earth—because he is a God of renewal, redemption, and transformation—then our present earthly endeavors might not altogether be in vain. That idea shines new light on our daily work.[3]

Individualistic Lens

Another reason why we miss out on the spiritual importance of daily work is our tendency to interpret the Bible through an individualistic lens. We tend to read the Bible as if God speaks to us as individuals, which is partly true, but we also tend to overlook the fact that God is addressing communities beyond our own church community. In his book *Work in the Spirit: Toward a Theology of Work*, Croatian Protestant theologian Miroslav Volf questions this type of thinking:

> Conservative Christians in the Western world prefer the combination "evangelism and market," to the combination "planning and market" that I am suggesting. This reflects their dislike for structural change and their enthusiasm for individual change. I have no quarrel with what they affirm (the need for individual change), but I do with what they deny (the need for structural change and for planning). With them I want to stress the importance of individual change not only for restoring a person's relation to God but also for enabling a proper operation of the economy.[4]

---

3. See Darrell Cosden, *The Heavenly Good of Earthly Work* (Grand Rapids: Baker Academic, 2006).

4. Miroslav Volf, *Work in the Spirit: Toward a Theology of Work* (Eugene, OR: Wipf & Stock, 2001), 20.

Summary

Business as Mission thrives on the waves generated by the Theology of Work (TOW) movement. TOW again is another expression of a broader movement seeking God's kingdom, where the whole gospel applies to all areas of life. It is a return to the Jewish roots of Christianity, with a more holistic mind-set. Although the Western worldview tends to be individualistic, there is a growing realization that in the Bible God addresses entire communities, desiring justice and redemption here and now for individuals, communities, and structures. Meanwhile, there is hope in our hearts that God will redeem some of our earthly efforts, weaving this into his eternal story. As Canadian theologian Michael Coheen says, "We must remain in the biblical world, discover the meaning of our lives there and fit our lives in line with this eternal plan."[5]

---

5. Michael W. Coheen, *The Urgency of Reading the Bible as One Story in the 21st Century* (lecture, Regent College, Vancouver BC, November 2, 2006).

Corrie Acorda-De Boer (Philippines)
Teaching Kidpreneurship in Manila's Slums

Corrie (second from right) celebrating a student's achievement
at one of their schools. (Photo courtesy of Vinnie Petti)

A curriculum for "Kidpreneur" has been developed and launched in the slums of Metro Manila. "We need to create new social movements in order to end poverty," says Dr. Corrie Acorda-De Boer, cofounder of Mission Ministries Philippines (MMP). Among the poor, this mission has helped start more than one thousand early childhood preschools and programs, as well as holistic-oriented churches. Over time, entrepreneurship has become part of the DNA of this mission; teaching children is a natural next step.

The Kidpreneur principles were first taught in one of the preschools established by Mission Ministries Philippines (http://missionministriesphilippines.org/page/kidpreneur) in partnership with a local Christian academy. The idea of teaching entrepreneurship concepts to four- to six-year-old children was pioneered by professors Rene and Anji Resurreccion, the founders of this particular school. While Rene was pursuing his master's degree in development studies in the Netherlands, the couple first started toying with the idea. Back in the Philippines, Anji integrated ideas she picked up from the German experiential learning model (called CEFE) for teaching enterprise to children. In the school Rene and Anji established, the children made toys and food "products," and were encouraged to sell them to friends and family, even as they learned about handling money and the basics of profit, saving, and investing.

"I visited their school together with the director of MMP, Chonabelle Domingo," shares Corrie. "The kids showed us how much money they had made from organizing a rummage sale, by baking cookies, or by making and selling toys. When we saw the excitement and satisfaction in the children's eyes as they shared how much money they had saved, we were inspired and we envisioned all our schools to have a Kidpreneur curriculum." So, together with Anji, MMP developed the curriculum further and introduced it in 2017 to all the preschools with which they currently have partnerships.

Faith-Based Social Movement

It might well become a faith-based social movement in the slums of Manila, as the possibility of tens of thousands of kids begin learning about entrepreneurship and are stimulated to use that gifting, while still attending any of the thousand-plus schools established by Mission Ministries Philippines in cooperation with local churches, NGOs, and seminaries. Generally, twenty to fifty children attend these schools, with some schools having between a hundred to three hundred children after they expanded into elementary and high schools.

Corrie says, "At a young age they learn how to think entrepreneurially and how to make money. Besides the basics of business, we give much attention to biblical character traits and use the stories of famous entrepreneurs who display these traits as examples."

"We base entrepreneurial activities on the belief that God is involved in our spiritual as well as our material lives."

Although some of the missionaries involved in the schools needed time to adapt to the idea of entrepreneurship, the people living in the slums adapted quickly. "The poor accept and pick it up right away, since it is their day-to-day need," Corrie explains. "We base entrepreneurial activities on the belief that God is involved in our spiritual as well as our material lives. God created us to be his coworkers; he wants us to steward his creation and desires *shalom* for families and communities. He wants to elevate us from poverty and desires for us to live in peace, prosperity, and productivity."

Mission Ministries Philippines

Mission Ministries Philippines was founded in the early eighties with a vision to end poverty. North American Stewart De Boer, Corrie's husband, was one of the initiators. Corrie, born and raised in the Philippines, was involved from the start and became its first director. They decided to focus on early childhood education, as well as on higher education, to be able to generate transformational leaders. From the beginning, instead of aiming to build a large mission organization, MMP concentrated on catalyzing and growing social movements by using principles of vision casting, collaboration, and partnership, while outsourcing some of the needed work.

Academia

The De Boers and other MMP staff are closely linked with Asian Theological Seminary. Stewart worked at this seminary as academic dean, president, and professor, while Corrie worked closely with students and the faculty for urban transformation. With the staff and the faculty, they developed curriculum to empower high school graduates in the slums—whether they were mothers, single people, or Sunday school teachers—helping them become competent preschool teachers.

Meanwhile MMP received help and inspiration from international universities—such as Azusa Pacific University (APU) and Bakke Graduate University (BGU), both based in the United States—to pioneer and catalyze the master of arts in transformational urban leadership and doctor in ministry in transformational leadership. In the Philippines, Corrie, Dr. Viv Grigg, and Dr. Ray Bakke pioneered these programs along with urban ministry colleagues, while involving other educational institutions in the nation and abroad. MMP still works closely with them and with universities in Asia (such as Bethel Seminary in Hong Kong), as they want to pass on what has been learned in the Philippines and help equip leaders globally to work among the poor.

A Journey from Dependency to Entrepreneurship

When the De Boers noticed that the support for the ministry was slowly dropping due to "donor fatigue," their interest for entrepreneurship started with a search to become more sustainable as a mission. Late in 2003, Stewart, already in his seventies, enrolled to study social entrepreneurship with the aim to become independent as a mission from foreign funding within seven years.

They looked at different models, and finally chose to produce and publish their own childhood education workbooks and teacher manuals, as this fit best with their mission's vision, goals, and talents. Later, they started a tour enterprise for foreign students and others interested, offering them a chance to experience life in the slums among the urban poor. The profits kept them in the black, and also helped expand their influence and serve a broader base. Initially, though, the change in the way of funding did not go easily and smoothly; some of the staff were not trained in business or equipped to handle new tasks such as outsourcing technical and marketing jobs. Some also were uncomfortable becoming involved in business, as they felt it was not the ministry as they were used to, preferring to expect God's provision through traditional ways. Corrie says, "It meant some mind shifting for some of our staff. We wanted to create a solid biblical foundation; we studied Scripture and were given modules by other theological universities, like the Theology of Work curriculum of Bakke Graduate University. Through research and study, we grew in understanding that God himself is entrepreneurial. We are created in his image, and we wanted to embrace this part of who God is."

Through choosing the approach of vision casting, collaboration, and partnership, MMP became a catalyst for a grassroots, faith-based social movement in the slums. Now, MMP is increasingly becoming a catalyst for developing social entrepreneurship. Not only children in marginalized situations, but the country as a whole could benefit from education that encourages entrepreneurship. Filipinos are globally known and hired for their service-oriented work, and many have to leave the country because they can't find a job at home. "Over 2,500 people leave each day to go serve in other nations," says Corrie. "This is breaking families apart and causing social problems, since many of them have partners and children they leave behind. Within our culture we are not used to consider-ing developing our business potential, but we must start recognizing such talents and encourage children to develop them. Our country has rich resources—like gold, silver, and copper—and we are blessed with fertile land. We need business activities which create jobs, so we don't have to go work abroad to support our families."

Social Entrepreneurship in the Slums

MMP is becoming increasingly involved itself in social entre-preneurship activities in the slums. One of the initiatives it started is a manpower agency linking unemployed youth to companies. "We saw the need for jobs," Corrie explains, "so we started a manpower service for a small fee. For example, a Chinese trader needed people to promote toys in different stores, a construction company needed painters and carpenters, and a restaurant owner chefs and waiters. We know people with potential in the slums and connect them with businesses."

Meanwhile, MMP also uses this network and influence to stim-ulate, connect, and facilitate bigger business start-ups, such as a company that makes environmentally friendly briquettes (charcoal), used for cooking. The interest for such endeavors is growing, both locally and internationally. "Recently, I met with Americans who are interested in investing in the slums," shares Corrie. "They have agricultural enzymes that help bind bricks and briquettes. That's big; that would be a whole other level of business!"

God Has Also Gifted the Poor

"We know that it is not easy to work with the poorest of the poor," admits Corrie. "I'm aware of the thought that they 'always need help,' and there is some truth to that. We should realize that they live in garbage dumps, are vulnerable and often mentally drained. They are also at the mercy of disasters; whole communities here in the Philip-pines have been wiped out through floods. Because of such disasters, our mission has lost much of the money we had lent through mi-crofinancing. But through these loans, we have seen people coming out of the garbage dumps. God has also gifted the poor."

Mission Ministries Philippines has seen results. Partnering with other organizations added to strength and innovation, including the area of entrepreneurship. For example, a sister organization, Companion with the Poor (CWTP), was pioneered by land rights lawyer Dr. Raineer Chu. CWTP has raised teams of entrepreneurial church planters to establish churches among the poorest of the poor, developing curriculum to empower missionaries to be tentmakers. Together with organizations like these, MMP dreams to raise children to become wealth creators, job generators, and foundation leaders.

> *"We have one billion very desperate people in the world. We need to rally businesspeople and help them develop vision and strategy to end poverty."*

Although it is challenging for Corrie and her team, they see opportunities come their way for the benefit of vulnerable communities, and they believe that entrepreneurship—Business as Mission—is on God's heart, both in the Philippines and beyond. Corrie passionately shares her vision: "We have one billion very desperate people in the world. We need to rally businesspeople and help them develop vision and strategy to end poverty. We need to disciple transformational leaders among the poor and the powerful, invest in educating the church, and develop curriculum for seminaries to understand how to transform cities."

> *"We need a new social movement. Let's teach kids at a young age that business is also God's mission, that they can be wealth creators and job providers."*

Corrie continues, "We need a new social movement. Let's teach kids at a young age that business is also God's mission, that they can be wealth creators and job providers. Business as Mission is on God's agenda."

Chapter 3

From Donating to Investing

Down the Ladder, in Touch with Brokenness

By Gea Gort

God in Jesus came to live among us. God didn't drop the gospel on a parachute from heaven, nor did he magically transform human beings, the earth, and everything there is. As a relational God, he sent his Son to live as a human being among us. Jesus came, as it were, "down the ladder" and ate, drank, and laughed with us. He also knew our brokenness and was touched by it.

In most cultures, the thinking still prevails, "Guys, girls, get up that ladder! Go for better, bigger, richer." In past decades, it seemed that in many places around the world people were indeed able to move ahead. In the meantime, we must acknowledge that ambition alone is not enough, especially as we see people and people groups falling off that ladder. Life can be complicated. Furthermore, over the past decades, we have thought that the modern zeitgeist with its big ideologies—such as capitalism, socialism, and science—would solve the world's problems. This zeitgeist has had its influence on Christian worldviews around the globe: "Follow Jesus, live according to biblical principles, and everything will be all right. Your life will be better, bigger, and richer." Of course, there is truth to that, since we serve a good God who wants the best for us. Many Christians are rediscovering, however, another part of the truth: following Jesus means also going down the ladder with him. He invites us to be in touch with brokenness—both our own and our neighbor's.

Down the Ladder, in Touch with Brokenness

BAM practitioners often have a healthy dose of ambition, but they also know the importance of moving down the ladder. They know that giving finances or sharing the gospel out of a sense of superiority—*I know it and will help you!*—can come across as "dropping the Bible or a bag of money." With all good intentions, it is likely that it won't touch hearts but erect walls, as it can come across as simplistic, cold, or arrogant. Part of discipleship is following Jesus down the ladder. That means first and foremost entering the brokenness of our own lives: recognizing it and bringing it into the light before God and people we trust. When we have been touched ourselves by his loving grace, we are better equipped to pass this love and grace on to others.

From Donating to Investing

Internationally, there is a trend away from donating toward investing. In my part of the world, Western Europe, the perception is that money is running out (whether this is true or not, I'm not sure, since we still live in one of the richest parts of the world). But economic systems have become shaky; the Western European welfare state is reigning itself in and evaluating the giving of aid to developing countries. These developments cause a paradigm shift, which could be summed it up as "from donating to investing."[1]

This trend could be typified as moving "down the ladder," since not only (lack of) finances is causing this shift, but also a change in thinking about development and aid—aid to both developing countries and needy people in Western vulnerable neighborhoods. Even though aid will always be needed for the poorest of the poor, the underlying thought is that "giving donations puts people in a position of dependency." This belief is not only growing in the West, but people in the developing world prefer empowerment above aid. This trend leads to a more businesslike approach of governments.

---

1. Source: Rien van Gendt, an international authority in the field of philanthropy and chair of the Society of Equity Funds in the Netherlands (FIN). For further reading, see particularly the transition from charity to strategic philanthropy (6) and "from donations to investment" (9), in "Foundations and Society: Sliding Panels" (lecture 2016), http://www.culturalfoundation.eu/library /foundations-and-society-sliding-panels-rien-van-gendt-lecture.

Aid and mission organizations are also catching on and moving toward business as a means to advance development.

Empowerment and Ownership

Even though the Bible encourages giving, there is also much biblical support for the idea of investment, empowerment, and ownership. Think of the parable of the talents, where the master entrusted his servants with bags of gold (Matt. 25:14–30). Similarly, after his resurrection, Jesus ascended to the Father. He gave us a mandate but also the Holy Spirit as an awesome Resourcer—the encourager who empowers us to follow in Jesus' footsteps. God gives ownership—responsibility and decision-making freedom— and meanwhile, he partners with us and calls us his friends.

We might sometimes wish for someone to tell us what to do, or for instant solutions instead of time-consuming and difficult processes. By wishing this, however, we might miss out on a meaningful journey, which is a part of having ownership. Ownership that brings joy is the theme of Dennis Bakke's book *Joy at Work*. "A joy-filled workplace gives people the freedom to use their talents and skills for the benefit of society, without being crushed or controlled by autocratic supervisors."[2] God is not an autocratic master. He wants us to mature while taking responsibility, so we can enjoy ownership for our own lives and for our communities.

Summary

No one promised us an easy ride. This is true as well for Business as Mission. The people engaged in BAM don't avoid brokenness. They go down the ladder into the mud and chaos, as Mats addresses in his chapter "Business as Mission Can Be Smelly." BAMers invest themselves in people and communities, in faith that their endeavors will bear fruit in due time. Their aim is to stand eye to eye with people, as they believe that through developing loving and trusting relationships, the way is paved for partnership, empowerment, and the joy of ownership.

---

2. Dennis W. Bakke, *Joy at Work: A Revolutionary Approach to Fun on the Job* (Seattle: PVG, 2005), 19.

Randy White (Fresno, California)
Building a Faith-Based Social Business Movement in the City

Randy (left) with the initiator of Tree of Life Fresno, an urban café and bakery downtown centered on renewal and restoration. They employ and coach people recovering from addictions.

Randy White initiated a social business movement in Fresno, California—with success. Desperate about the needs in their city, Christians came together. Then a probing question from their mayor, Ashley Swearengin, ignited new business activities. She asked church leaders, "What role do faith institutions play in the economic well-being of our city?" This question stimulated the conversation, leading to theological and empirical research, to publications, and finally to action.

One of the activities is the so-called Spark Tank. This is a yearly festive event, where churches, nonprofit organizations, and social entrepreneurs in Fresno can present their ideas while a committee evaluates the business plans according to a triple bottom line: Is it financially sustainable, does it address a social need or employ people with barriers, and is it adding to the environmental health of the valley? Financial awards are given to promising ventures. The Spark Tank started in 2012, and within the first four years they helped start thirty-two start-ups and expect to help another twenty over the next two years.

"Start-ups are given a platform," explains Randy, "and we assist in finding mentoring, training, and investment. Our aim is to build a social business movement, and in order to do so, it is essential to see models of Christ-centered economic development."

Social Business Examples

In 2015, Spark Tank awarded and supported the Tree of Life Fresno (http://www.treeoflifefresno.com). This fresh farm-to-table café serves local agricultural products, while also providing meaningful employment to men and women who have completed drug and alcohol rehabilitation.

In other ways, the place is a symbol of healing and renewal. Through adaptive reuse of materials, the interior is creatively decorated and the café brings liveliness to downtown Fresno—an area that had previously been suffering from neglect. Clients from the surrounding offices have taken notice and are coming back for their lunchtimes because of the atmosphere, home-cooked food, and reasonable prices.

Other examples of BAM businesses in the area are Rock Pile Yard Service, which employs men coming out of prison, and Crumb 'n Get 'Em Cupcakes, which employs young teenagers in a high poverty neighborhood. Randy says, "Churches and organizations build relationships this way with vulnerable young people and speak into their lives, while helping them earn some money."

Business start-ups are risky, and roughly half of them don't make it. Social enterprises face even more challenges to survive financially. Fresno's social entrepreneurs, however, have a decent success rate. "A third goes very well," says Randy. "Another third is iffy. Sometimes an idea needs time to grow." This is the case with a coffee and pastry bar initiative. The social and gospel element of this bar is to create jobs for at-risk youth while working and connecting with them. The initiator, a young entrepreneur, was planning to use his parents' restaurant as a base, but the plan has evolved beyond that. Recently, a building became available to start his coffee and pastry bar right across from a high school. "We didn't hear from him for two years," says Randy, "but now it's an even larger effort than originally planned."

Background

Fresno's 500,000 inhabitants are definitely in need of these types of businesses that provide jobs for them: the city is second in the

United States on the list of highest rate of concentrated poverty. As the city is located in an agricultural area, it attracts many migrants—the working poor. Randy sees firsthand how this has an effect on people.

In the 1990s, he moved with his family to one of the worst neighborhoods in town, because they believed that the gospel is about God's saving grace, a grace that can also be applied to a challenging neighborhood. Others followed suit and a leadership network developed of Christians caring for their city. In those years, Fresno faced a major problem with crime: Nine thousand gang members were responsible for over a hundred murders a year. "Desperation drove us together," shares Randy. Meanwhile the number of murders has been cut by about half, and Fresno is an example in the US of Christians working together to seek the transformation of their city.

> *"Business needs to be an integrated part*
> *of community transformation."*

Randy played a key role in this movement. He initiated, networked, and supported these businesses, but he also reflected and developed a theological framework. As a result, Fresno Pacific University asked him to teach, set up, and lead its Center for Community Transformation (http://cctfresno.org). Through years now of involvement, Randy is more than ever convinced that business needs to be an integrated part of community transformation.

Reflection and Stories

To tackle the question of why a church or nonprofit should go into business, Randy edited *The Work of Our Hands: Faith-Rooted Approaches to Job, Creation, Training, or Placement in a Context of Concentrated Poverty* (Condeo Press, 2012), which he produced in cooperation with Fresno Pacific University. Besides basic theological reflection on the subject, it contains examples of faith-rooted job creation, training, and placement. Over one thousand books were distributed to leaders of churches and nonprofits, as well as to the city council members and four hundred businesspeople. Mayor Ashley Swearengin wrote the preface, and the book is dedicated to those in Fresno who have the right to the dignity of working.

Building a Movement

The yearly Spark Tank, as mentioned, provided initiatives a platform, and the rewards provided a monetary reason to try. Meanwhile, connections were made with existing organizations to structure needed support, as they did with a volunteer business organization. As a result, retired businesspeople are now involved and lead business courses. Randy also saw the importance for this movement to be anchored in a neutral institution: "Fresno Pacific University provides such an anchor. That gives trust and validates."

Randy knows that building a social business movement is quite a journey. "Christian businesspeople tend to think: 'I pray for lunch, go to church, and might plan a Bible study in my office,' but they may not be used to the idea of using their business as a vehicle for kingdom purposes. Many pastors on the other hand have the tendency to think that money and business are bad and have nothing to do with church."

Paradigm shifts and new insights are therefore needed. For example, it is a fact that a church is not the only place to share faith but also an economic engine. It is a social group that has people on its payroll, provides daycare for kids and lunches in the neighborhood, and gets the church roof repaired. In Pennsylvania, it was calculated that eleven churches, with attendants ranging from three hundred to seven thousand, yearly contributed 50.5 million dollars to the local economy. Randy says, "When we realize this, our perspectives change."

Changing Perspectives

Randy believes that when our perspectives change, we are better able to see opportunities before us. He gives an example of how a church could expand on the fact of "being an economic engine" by using their physical assets: "A single mom can make tamales in her kitchen, but she could make much more in a church kitchen down the street. A bit more income enables her to pay for her kid's school tuition or double her living space. This way, churches can empower people and become a tangible blessing in their cities and neighborhoods."

> *"People are not prone to try new things, unless*
> *there is a deep dissatisfaction."*

Randy knows that change takes time. "People are not prone to try new things, unless there is a deep dissatisfaction—'a holy discontent with the way things are,' as Bill Hybels says." The huge needs in Fresno feed this dissatisfaction, and a growing number of people are becoming aware of the potential of merging business and mission. Randy: "We are starting to see social business as just another way to minister, an alternate approach to carrying out our mission of transformation. As the Spirit of God brings this transformation to individual lives, we see what Dr. Martin Luther King often repeated—that transformed people can transform a society."

Joe White (Fresno, California)

A Church Based on Business—A Way to Get Entangled with the Neighborhood

Joe and Heidi White. (Photo courtesy of Kevin Rees)

"Business is an on-ramp to our church," says Pastor Joe White. He is working together with the people of the neighborhood to seek its welfare. Tangible and practical. To create a legal framework to serve this purpose, he started a business and a foundation. A Sunday meeting with the people involved is just one of the parts of the total package.

The Sunday gathering is flourishing. In early 2016, two people started this endeavor in a predominantly Hispanic neighborhood in Fresno. Nine months later, sixty people now participate in the Sunday gatherings. They are all living and daily involved in the neighborhood. Joe counts twenty-one initiatives "their people" are involved in during the week through business, politics, or nonprofit organizations.

This Neighborhood Is My Parish

Joe called the church gathering Neighborhood Church Fresno (http://www.neighborhoodchurchfresno.com). This is because he has a strong sense of a "theology of place" and looks at the 953 houses of the neighborhood as "his parish." He envisions his church to become totally entangled with the daily lives of the local people. To ensure they stay on track, he has attached a legal agreement to businesses and nonprofits that they will hire only people from the neighborhood and be involved in activities to strengthen it.

A Natural Way of Evangelism and Discipleship

Business as Mission is an important part of his church model. Business is not another thing to add to a busy church life; it creates economic opportunities for the neighborhood. Joe views it as an on-ramp to his church and therefore considers it as an effective evangelistic and discipleship tool. "It gives us ongoing connections with people and keeps us engaged with them, because business provides daily structure. While we work together, we can live out what it means to be a Christian. That means that during the week evangelism and discipleship take place in a natural way."

Keep It Simple

"Keep it simple" is Joe's advice. "At first we were planning to start a sandwich shop, but it took too much of our time and involvement. It became demotivating for us." Now they are looking for simple, win-win business opportunities. Because they wanted to be in contact with the youth of the neighborhood, they started a repair service to support this aim: "We hire youth for minimum wages to do repairs on homes. We meet with the youth weekly and plan every month a time to train them in specific specialty jobs, like how to repair the windows in this neighborhood, which are often broken. We are like an agent, and it gives us connections with the homeowners of our neighborhood. It is a win-win situation."

They are also in the middle of launching a compost business. A plot of land was made available to them, where they have put compost bins. They have contacted gardeners in the area, who have had to pay to dispose of their greens, and offered to dump their greens for free. Meanwhile, they teach young people how to make compost, which can be sold in time.

Use All Skills and All Genders

Embracing BAM gives church members more opportunities to actively participate, where both male and female are encouraged to use their professional and business skills. "It levels the playing field," Joe says. "In most churches there is a gender divide. Wealthy men are overutilized and are asked to be on boards and in leadership roles, while females, who might own businesses, are at the door and serving coffee. We want to utilize all skills of all genders."

> *"There is no movement without friction.*
> *I decided to embrace the friction."*

Joe admits that he is entrepreneur who doesn't shy away from shaking things up. For church planters, it would generally feel quite natural to start businesses since they are more entrepreneurial by nature, while pastors of existing churches tend to be more pastoral. In the church as a whole, however, Joe thinks we can use a bit of rethinking: "The reason why churches take people on mission trips is to encourage them to step out of their comfort zones. When we step out, we move and we change. Movement and change is uncomfortable, but it does shake things up—in individual lives but also in neighborhoods, because I view movement in a neighborhood as a commitment to innovation and innovation is at the heart of Jesus' promise of renewal. But we better realize that there is no movement without friction. I decided to embrace that friction, because I want to move my area of influence from *the way things are* to *the way things could be* because Jesus is promising to make all things new—all things: spiritually, physically, socially, and economically."[3]

---

3. For more information, watch this two-minute video: https://vimeo .com/145942563.

CHAPTER 4

EMBRACING THE LOCAL IN A GLOBAL WORLD

Toward a Theology of Place

By Gea Gort

"Think global, act local" is a phrase often heard in business strategy, where multinational corporations are encouraged to root locally. "Living glocal" is another expression that converges the words *global* and *local*. Global involvement is encouraged in the Bible, as we are summoned to take the gospel to the ends of the earth. But living in a global time frame, we need to remember to root and get entangled in the lives of people where we live and work, as Joe White graphically expressed it in the last story. Although globalization has brought amazing opportunities, the pendulum is swinging back and there is renewed appreciation of the local: local production, consumption, and interaction. God created us with a desire to bond and belong to people and places. He modeled a missional way of life: incarnational living. God came to earth and revealed himself in a certain time and place.

Theology of Place

Theologically there is also a re-appreciation of the importance of place. One of my professors, Ray Bakke, used to live and work as a Baptist pastor in the inner city of Chicago. While fellow Christians of that time moved to the well-to-do outskirts of the city, he moved with his young family into the ghetto. This made him search the Bible, hence his encouragement to us to have a "Theology of Place."

We need to be aware of the importance of place and realize that a city is more than the amount of buildings and individuals—it has a personality.[1] Ray, as others before and after him, also discovered the value of the Roman Catholic perception of "parish." While evangelicals could have their church building anywhere and members could come from everywhere, the Roman Catholic priests perceived the whole neighborhood as their parish, not just the members of the church.

Relocation

Similar is the movement that became known as "relocation" in the 1980s. Christians, such as Randy White and his family, moved to a particular and oftentimes needy neighborhood, bought a house, befriended neighbors, and built networks in the neighborhood in a grassroots effort to build social cohesiveness within the community. It's about looking people in the face, appreciating minor changes and not despising the day of the small beginnings. Relocators like to quote John 1:14 from The Message: "The Word became flesh and blood and moved into the neighborhood." God made himself known in the context of a particular place, time, and culture. He came and had an address.

Bonding and Belonging

In societies where people seem to be "all over the place" and individualism has gone too far, there remains the human desire to bond with and belong to a certain group and place. Through the incarnation—God becoming human in Jesus—God chose to belong to a certain family, village, and people group. Bonding and belonging are also pictured through the image of the Triune God: Father, Son, and the Holy Spirit in perfect love, mutual appreciation, and equality. Christian faith is about connecting, belonging, and bond-

---

1. As described for example in Ezekiel 16:46, where God speaks to Jerusalem as to a person: "Your older sister was Samaria, who lived to the north of you with her daughters." For more about "theology of place," see Gea Gort, "Commitment to the Place," *God in the City: A Missional Way of Life in an Urban Context* (Harmond Press, 2012), ch. 6.

ing. We are invited to do so with the Triune God and with the local and global church. From there, belonging can be offered to others. We are not to be on a solely individual spiritual journey; Christian faith is also about the transformation and renewal of institutions, neighborhoods, and cities. That means becoming "entangled" with people and places. The authors of *The New Parish: How Neighborhood Churches Are Transforming Mission, Discipleship, and Community* warn that a Western globalized and individual mind-set might disregard the value of being connected to a certain place and therefore be in danger to "live above place." They point out, "If the nature of God as Trinity models your relational calling, then the incarnation of God demonstrates your missional calling to live into time and place."[2]

Business as Mission companies can respond to this missional call, and the human need to bond and belong, both with people and place. Building a business means long-term commitment, and in many cases close involvement with our immediate environments. As many stories illustrate, BAM can help build the local community through services that connect people with one another within the neighborhood—connecting in a nonthreatening way with other believers, other cultures, or nonbelievers of a post-Christian generation.

BAM values belonging and bonding as expressed in its value "in community, for community," since a company can also offer people the possibility of becoming part of a business community. Within a neutral setting of a business, trust and relationship can flourish, exchanges about faith can become natural, and it can become a place where God is experienced. We will look further at this in the next chapter.

Summary

Business as Mission is glocal—it is both global and local. BAM is a global movement; being globally connected can be inspirational and beneficial in various ways. But BAM is also about a

---

2. Paul Sparks, Tim Soerens, and Dwight J. Friesen, *The New Parish: How Neighborhood Churches are Transforming Mission, Discipleship, and Community* (Downers Grove, IL: IVP Books, 2014), 26.

commitment to a place: to a neighborhood, city, and country. Businesses as Mission can be places of connection and belonging, building social cohesiveness through rooting and building relationships locally, and embracing their locality while learning about their particular personalities. Not living "above place" but getting entangled locally. Bonding, belonging, and appreciating the value of the place to which we are called, as God "moved into the neighborhood" and made himself known within the setting of a certain time and place.

Project Developer Norbert Tews (Berlin)
Community Center Serves Upper-Class Neighborhood

In a trendy neighborhood in the inner city of Berlin, a building project of 2,400 square meters has been realized, becoming the home of a community center: Haus C13. They serve the neighborhood through a holistic and integrated approach to education, health, and family. Norbert Tews decided to take responsibility so a vision could become reality: "We learned to follow in what God had prepared."

The center is located in the trendy neighborhood Prenzlauer Berg. The famous Bernauer Strasse, where people jumped off the wall in the days of communism, is part of the neighborhood. Working class Eastern Berliners used to live here, but nowadays most of its ninety thousand inhabitants are creative professionals. In this area, an empty space became available when a building—which had been damaged in World War II and had never been rebuilt—came up for sale. Norbert Tews heard about this piece of land, as he was involved with an evangelical elementary school in the neighborhood. An idea sparked in his mind: Could this be used for God's kingdom?

Norbert brought some people together who researched the neighborhood, questioning and praying what could be done with this plot of land. A vision started to develop as they realized that many of the young creative professionals living in this neighborhood have "patchwork families": children out of former relationships. Serving these families, who have to deal with various issues, became one of the keys to connect with the neighborhood. A foundation was formed in order to realize the vision to live and work together in an integrated and holistic way, while giving the neighborhood a positive incentive in the areas of education, health, and family, supported with art and culture. They called the foundation *Bildung, Werte, Leben* (education, values, life; www.bildung-werte-leben.de). "People don't realize that we first started with the vision," Norbert says. "Often it is the other way around. A foundation will decide what they will do. We started with the vision, after researching what would be fitting in this area."

The Building

The vision became reality when the doors of the center opened in 2013. More than forty people who share the vision now live and/or work here. The spacious building has 2,400 square meters (about 25,800 square feet) and six floors. On the ground floor is a café on the street side, and behind it is a hall that can be rented by different groups for gatherings such as art shows, concerts, or church services. In the back part of the building is a kindergarten. The top floors have apartments of different sizes to house members, while the various spaces in the middle floors are rented out to Christian health practitioners in areas of ergo- and physiotherapy, pediatrics, maternity, child and youth psychotherapy, as well as singles, couples, and family therapy.

Integrated and Holistic

"These professionals are excited that they can combine mission with their profession," says Norbert. "They often felt divided, because in Germany it's hard to integrate faith in areas of therapy and healthcare. It is just not done."

Norbert himself, who always felt a tension between his technical and social interests, could also integrate these two areas in which he studied and worked. The result can be seen: the building stands out in the streets of Berlin because of its spacious, transparent, and inviting structure, and has already been awarded several times for its architecture. "We wanted the architecture to support the vision."

A Call to Take Responsibility

The total cost was seven million euro. One-third of the budget was raised through the foundation, a third covered through the sale of the apartments, and the other third by a loan from the bank. Meanwhile, the project is self-sustaining through the income from the rental of office space, the theater, and the café/lunchroom. The project took seven years to realize—from the moment the small group first met to discuss the vision, to the opening. "Someone challenged me to make the vision a reality," shares Norbert. "It won't just happen by itself. I felt a call from God to take responsibility."

Intentionally Following Christ: Slow Down, Seek Quiet, and Reflect

The seven years, however, have been a long, bumpy, and at times lonely road. "There were endless challenges," recalls Norbert. "I learned to intentionally follow Christ. Before I used to walk in front of God, and pray that God would bless what I did, but I have learned to slow down and ask: 'God, where are you working? How can I enter into what you are doing?' It's about fleshing out what God wants to give to us, while waiting and walking into what he has prepared."

During that time, Norbert would take one day a month to go away and seek quiet. That wasn't easy and he needed to fight for that time, but those days became crucial for him: "It's about coming into a purpose-free area. For me this meant walking and writing to empty my head and thoughts; allowing stillness, receiving from God, while reflecting and discerning."

Meanwhile, the project is running well and connections with people from the neighborhood are developing. Norbert has happily given the lead over to others to further build and develop the work. Recently, he has been asked to help envision and develop a project in another neighborhood, together with a local church and a well-to-do businessman. He sees the potential of a fruitful combination: a graying and seeking church and a businessman who wants to leave a legacy for the community that is asking for help from visionaries and project developers to find new ways to share the gospel. This next project might look similar or different. It depends on what fits that neighborhood and situation.

"Don't let your history determine what you are going to do, but let God determine."

Looking back, Norbert is grateful for all that has come to pass so far. He is a bit amazed that he played a key role in pulling it off. The whole project started with an idea, but there wasn't any money. Norbert has an ordinary Eastern German background and was the first one to study in his family: "It's not in my history and biography to do something like this size: a project of seven million! Receiving encouragement was not part of my upbringing, and I'm not a typical go-getter either. But God needed someone to be willing to take responsibility. Through it all I learned, 'Don't let your history determine what you are going to do, but let God determine. Don't identify with your past, but with God's future.'"

Church Planter Johannes van den Akker (Amsterdam)

A Contemporary Monastery Starts a Brewery

"The Clay Cloister [Dutch: Het Klei Klooster*] is located over there,"
points Johannes van den Akker. "In that apartment block." In a challenging neighborhood of southeast Amsterdam, a group of people
started a living and faith community. A city garden and a brewery are
part of the plan. This will enable the monastery to become financially
self-sufficient. But, equally important, these social businesses connect
them with the neighborhood.*

At the beginning of 2015, several families, couples, and singles
with a variety of church backgrounds started a contemporary monastery, the Clay Cloister (http://kleiklooster.nl). Eight apartments in
need of refurbishment were purchased and renovated. These apartments are located in a T-shape on the first and second floors, in the
middle of the apartment block. The entrance to the chapel is on the
first floor, and the top floor has a community room, guest quarters,
and homes.

The residents seek the welfare of the neighborhood. "We want to
offer hospitality, but we aim for more than just 'helping neighbors,'"
shares Johannes van den Akker, the initiator. "Besides the horizon-
tal, social aspect, we want to create space for the vertical dimension."

How Are We a Church?

"How to connect Sunday and Monday?" is the quest that led to the plans for a monastery, brewery, and city garden. Although the group is connected with an innovative church planting movement, they didn't want to start a new church—since in this multicultural part of southeast Amsterdam already over a hundred churches exist. Yet somehow these churches mainly stay within their own circles and don't seem to influence the neighborhood. Therefore, Johannes's group purposely looked for other ways "to be church." He knew they had to develop another church model, since he saw from his own experience that it is easy to have good intentions while not knowing how to make them concrete. "Within church circles we confess faith in a cognitive way. We talk about concepts like charity, justice, and hospitality. But these concepts seem to stay in our heads; all too often the values we believe in don't get hands and feet. We therefore decided that we wanted to make them concrete and relevant by creating a setting in which it can take place in a natural way. For example, I want my children to experience hospitality, that it will be normal for them to have total strangers over for dinner. When people knock on the door of our community we want to open the door; we want to look lonely people in the eye, but that means being available 24/7. As a single family we cannot sustain such hospitality, but as a group we can. As members of our community we can also sharpen, encourage, and hold each other accountable to our vision."

"We want to look lonely people in the eye."

Building intentionally on a network of relationships in the neighborhood is a part of this vision. Besides developing meaningful relationships themselves, once trust is built, they look for ways to connect acquaintances with other acquaintances. Johannes says, "A neighbor calls me sometimes. I have never talked about my faith with her, but recently she told me, 'I call you because I need to connect with our dear Lord.' She is lonely and knows hardly anyone. We are careful with her trust, but we aim at reconnecting people like her eventually with others in the area so their social network will grow." The Clay Cloister wants to contribute to quality of life in that quarter in a relational and organic way. The idea for social businesses—such as a brewery and city garden—fitted well within this vision.

Clay Beer

The first bottle of Clay Beer (http://brouwerijkleiburg.nl/over-ons) opened new doors when it was offered to the city district councilor at City Hall. This generated a lot of media attention and new contacts. "The local government embraces our initiative," says Johannes, "because it wants to portray southeast Amsterdam positively and likes to see local creative businesses emerge. Our initiative fits in that picture."

January 2017, the brewery opened its doors. The kettles are designed for a one-thousand-liter brewery. Johannes says, "The first years we want to produce fifty thousand liters of beer annually, and in five years' time over one hundred thousand. Our business plan is based on social entrepreneurship. We estimate that in a number of years our company will employ ten people. We also want to hire a few so-called drop-outs."

The Clay Cloister is one of the shareholders of the brewery. This enables them to become financially independent and repay their debt to the PKN (National Dutch Protestant Church) who financially invested in the Clay Cloister. "We shouldn't be dependent on grants," Johannes believes. "That creates laziness. We feel more ownership when we invest in the company ourselves, believe in it, and work hard for it."

Monastery Garden

Besides the brewery, the Clay Cloister sees potential in developing a city garden. The municipality granted them access to use an area the size of half a soccer field. "We will grow here hops for the brewery but also vegetables that we plan to sell in a small local marketplace." In the near future, the highway next to their apartment block will be covered with a two-kilometer-long roof, which will be developed as communal green space including a park and city garden. Johannes foresees potential. "Besides revenue models, a city garden offers opportunities for neighborhood participation. We have contacts with schools, community centers, and welfare clubs, and we offer educational and leisure programs for their people."

"Get started with your idea!"

Johannes is co-owner of a consultancy firm to help social start-ups. Although he is a theologically trained pastor, he "prefers to work in the margin of the church." He wants to develop a relevant story, while sharing and selling that story beyond Christian circles. "Drop your idea here and there, talk about it," says Johannes. "That's what I am doing, and people are picking it up. It forces me to communicate our vision with different people, but that sharpens me and makes my story stronger—much stronger than when I reduce faith experiences to the Christian context only. It is therefore my conviction that we, as Christians, should participate much more in society. So, dare to dream and get started with your idea!"

CHAPTER 5

IN COMMUNITY, FOR COMMUNITY

From Individualism to Community

By Gea Gort

If you have ever traveled through Western Europe, then you probably remember seeing church towers from afar. They were erected in the center squares of villages and cities. It is a visible sign that for a long time the church has been a central force within culture, and the place to be. Europe's Christianity has been exported and this might be one reason why many Christians view church as a centripetal force: God's Spirit calling and revealing him within a church setting. This is true, but the gospel is also a centrifugal force. BAM pioneers embrace this outgoing force. Instead of staying in the center, many of them go and set up a business to create opportunities to dine and fellowship with "the other" to make the gospel tangible out there.

From Individualism to Community

Within Christianity, both community and individualism are cherished. Individualism centers on personal salvation, cherishing a relationship with a personal God. But within a Western society, where individualism has gone too far, the motto of BAM—"in community, for community"—resonates with a growing number of people. Christians know that a community tends to have more impact than the witness of a single individual. A community could be a church, but also a group of people connected through a business as mission-type endeavor.

In Community, for Community

BAM regards "in community, for community" as one of its core values. "In community" is about building relationships within the company among colleagues, with the aim of creating a good work atmosphere. While relationships are challenged where the "rubber hits the road," and issues come up wherever people work together, BAMers regard them as opportunities for growth and discipleship, tangibly showing what it means to follow Christ. But business by nature is also outward looking (for community): building relationships with clients, customers, and suppliers; and serving the broader community through products and services with the aim of seeking the economic, social, ecological, and spiritual welfare of the community.

Coffee & Deeds

Business as Mission can inspire the church to find new ways to connect (more) with society. While BAM is not "the new church concept," it aims to be complementary to existing churches and can strengthen the local church. One such example is Coffee & Deeds in Zürich, Switzerland (http://coffee-deeds.ch). In a seemingly tranquil suburb, twenty-six-year-old Benjamin Bucher established a beautifully decorated café where they serve wonderful coffees and lunches. It is a high-quality lunchroom, located just across the street from a Reformed church. Benjamin grew up in this church and in this neighborhood, known as "the Bronx" of the city, where both rich and poor reside. During a year of traveling and working in Australia, Benjamin was touched by church events where many youth participated. While there, on the other side of the world, he developed a vision for both his own graying church and his neighborhood. Back home he joined a small group of Christians, who came from different churches in the neighborhood, to discuss how they could connect more with their neighbors. During discussions and prayer, the idea for Coffee & Deeds developed and Benjamin became the champion of the project: "We have created a place where good coffee and quality products are served within a beautiful, artsy ambiance. Through practical aid, we connect low and higher educated people. We just want to love the people in this community." This is all done in close cooperation with Benjamin's home church, since the lunchroom is located in a building owned by the church. Also, about half of his customers and volunteers are his fellow church members—older church folks who love and support the endeavor of this young man.

Significance of Institutions

We want to stress that religious institutions are important, as they have gathered wisdom throughout the ages and bring stability. Institutions help society to be organized and help provide order. Religious institutions are like deeply rooted trees, but around them, or sometimes far away from them, new initiatives can bring richness and versatility, springing up like little plants and flowers. Tree, plant, and flower each have its own role; when they come from the same Source, they can complement one another. Whether seekers will find something of that Source in a tree, plant, or flower is secondary. Together, through mutual encouragement and appreciation, the fertility of the soil is increased; through different expressions at different locations, love and justice can grow—places that point toward Christ. All this occurs in the knowledge that we depend on God's grace: his Spirit healing and touching hearts and encouraging us to act, in order to pass on the blessing.

Summary

BAM practitioners tend to be outward focused. They are on a journey to find connection with the social environments of different believers, in a desire to make God's kingdom tangible for them. From the perspective of "in community, for community" they connect, build relationships within their own community (business/church group), while aiming to include and serve the broader community. All this while embracing the outward force of the gospel: planting seeds sometimes far away from the tree, the institutional church, and other times flowering under its branches. All are needed—flowers, plants, and trees—as they can strengthen and complement one another.

Piet Brinksma (Amsterdam)
Church Denomination Moves toward a Holistic Perspective

"The perspective on being church is shifting," says Piet Brinksma, a Foursquare pastor in Amsterdam. "Business as Mission fits right into that shift." Piet is globally involved and witnessed blessing when church planters pursue peace and justice in their host countries. Also in his own Western setting, Piet sees the value of involvement with economic and social activities. It demands a holistic perspective, including entrepreneurship.

The Foursquare Church (http://www.foursquare.org) saw amazing things happening in Cambodia where its missionary, Ted Olbrick, is active (http://fcopi.org). Ted felt God telling him, "Take care of the widows and orphans, and I will take care of the church." "Ted founded orphanages," shares Piet Brinksma. "He is an entrepreneur so he acquired and developed rice paddy fields in the areas he visited. He had a professional background in rice research, and by the grace of God, Ted was able to assess which rice paddies had good potential. In the areas around the orphanages and agricultural businesses, churches and schools were constructed. The activities provided work, income, education, and food. Now, fifteen years later, there are over one hundred of those orphanage-compounds and over six thousand churches, which led more than one million people to Christ in Cambodia."

---

*"Their vision went further than church planting. . . .
They prioritized transformation; they wanted to
address the needs they were confronted with."*

"Leslie Keegel is another example of a holistic approach in Sri Lanka, his country of birth," continues Piet. "As a national leader of Foursquare, Leslie developed a vision that prioritizes the transformation of the island. Their vision went further than church planting, the amount of churches, or the development of a church organization. They prioritized transformation; they wanted to address the needs they were confronted with. Think of ethnical disparity, poverty, traumas caused by civil war, spiritual darkness, and a corrupt and incompetent government. As a result they gave consultations to government leaders, built houses, and started companies like chicken farms. At the moment, there are more than fifteen hundred Foursquare (home) churches in this country. In addition, we see a lot of signs and miracles in this Buddhist and spiritually sensitive country."

Foursquare Global

Globally, the Foursquare denomination has around one hundred thousand churches, with eight to ten million church members. Piet was a board member of the Foursquare Foundation and knows the stories mentioned above well, as he was involved in supporting mission projects of the Foursquare denomination around the globe. An analysis of the foundation's project evaluations showed that the most fruitful ones had a number of characteristics in common. "We noticed the importance of a holistic approach in projects: the pursuit of *shalom*—peace and justice—in all relevant areas of life. We also saw the positive effects of collaboration, of working together with other parties. Furthermore, a discipleship and church planting vision with an emphasis on the kingdom, while acknowledging the power of the Holy Spirit and his gifts and ministries, empowers us to live out his kingdom in all facets of life." This encompasses their perspective on work and business. "Those church planters did it intuitively," continues Piet. "Business as Mission was not a well-known term at the time, but its principles were part of their approach. BAM

fits with the DNA of Foursquare, and we have now incorporated it
explicitly as part of our international strategy."

"There is no need for church leaders to become entrepreneurs
themselves," says Piet. "But we can help spread the vision and view
the church as a breeding place where entrepreneurs connect and
where they receive support and inspiration. It is essential to encourage and develop talents like business and innovation within our
churches, besides pastoral and teaching talents."

Changing Perspectives on Mission and Being Church

Besides his international involvement, Piet is active in the city
of Amsterdam as a pastor and missional pioneer, as well as a leader
in citywide movements focusing on the *shalom* of the city. "Both in
our own missional activities as well as overall in the city, I see that
Christ inspired business activities—like social businesses, business
consultants, and civic organizations—to become a more intentional
part in the kingdom mission. It is a great way to connect Christ-
followers with the needs and assets of the city, but even more to
engage in serving relationships with those who have no connection
with the church or the gospel. Finally, business is a way to create
financial sustainability."

Piet sees BAM-related activities as a part of a bigger picture: the
church as a transforming power in neighborhoods and society. "As
a church denomination, we used to give much attention to growth
and wholeness of our individual members and their destiny. That's
a good thing: knowing who we are in Christ. But our focus is shifting toward including the wholeness of all aspects of life; we are
discovering what we, as a group and as a community of Christ, can
mean for the area where we are planted. It requires that we get to
know and love our neighborhoods, and find out what's going on. It
requires looking for connections with others who are already pursuing the good. God is already at work all around us—Calvin called
this common grace. We need to recognize and connect with what's
already there. In our case, we have a good collaboration with the
building manager, housing association, and with other influencers
in the area."

Piet views Business as Mission as one of the components of a
shift in the perspective on church and being church: "Generally

speaking, the church was regarded as the focal point in missionary thinking, but we see now a theological shift with Christ and the mission of God in this world at its core. From this core, Jesus' followers engage in mission, resulting in a group of people who put discipleship into practice, resulting in a 'church.' But it is much more of a fluid church. In China, I know of a church that functions within a factory, while in other places groups of people intermingle, en route inviting others while shaping God's kingdom."

Mandate: Developing Culture and Making Disciples

In the book of Genesis, God commands us to work the earth and develop the culture through bringing order, work, and beauty to the world, which is known as the "cultural mandate." Jesus tells us to make all nations his disciples, which means that the "culture mandate" becomes Jesus' mandate as well. Piet says, "As Christians we received the DNA of both mandates. From that kingdom perspective, planting churches and planting businesses go hand in hand."

Jonathan Hall (Florida/Brazil)

Weaving and Planting BAM within a Church Denomination

Jonathan Hall leads the Foursquare BAM Network (http://foursquare bam.com) and champions Business as Mission within his church denomination. In 2010, its leadership affirmed the BAM concept and gave the green light to introduce the concept within its circles. Through a relational and informal approach, there is now growing denominational interest while principles and concepts are spread. A BAM-focused business major has emerged at Life Pacific Bible College, and BAM is discussed at global leadership gatherings.

Jonathan Hall got the first "go ahead" from Glenn Burris, president of the Foursquare Church, and probably could have asked for a title, office, staff, and budget to introduce BAM to Foursquare, yet he chose another route. Jonathan began finding colleagues and leaders within the church family who were engaged or interested in BAM and began an informal network. "BAM is about a paradigm change, and that takes time," explains Jonathan. "We found other champions who are involved in BAM out of passion and calling, and we initiated a learning community. Our network attempts an imbedding at the ground level. That takes longer but is fruitful in the long run. At the same time we value the approval and affirmation of our top leadership for guidance and legitimacy."

Foursquare

Jonathan has served Foursquare from around the age of eighteen, and while now living in Florida, he and his wife lived most of their life in Brazil. He is an ideal "BAM champion" with both mission and business in his genes. When his parents were missionaries in Belo Horizonte and he was still in his teens, he was already importing Christian music into Brazil. Later in life, he oversaw Foursquare's missional activities in Brazil (where there are over twenty thousand churches) and South America. He later served as Foursquare vice president and director of missions, all the while encouraging entrepreneurial activities inside and outside of the church, especially among the "bottom billion." His personality, networking, and innovative abilities have increasingly given him a role and voice in the Foursquare family, and he is regarded as one of their "lifelong Foursquare innovators."

BAM Is Countercultural

While Jonathan emphasizes that he feels privileged to serve his church family, he also realizes that BAM and Theology of Work can be countercultural within established religious organizations. Jonathan explains: "In Latin America, for example, there is a strong Catholic heritage, which includes the tradition of the professional 'full-time' church clergy. This common and traditional model tends to elevate credentialed ministers, devalue talent in the pew, and promote a sacred-secular divide. A common underlying message heard in many congregations is that your 'secular' work is not that important, and just a necessary evil to be able to eat and tithe."

Jonathan thinks that a renewed view of work is needed. "Work and business are biblical and all about stewardship, human dignity, and sustainability. When we teach a biblical perspective on work, we also help pastors in many places in the world, as they need to work 'secularly' for their income, which is often viewed negatively. The number of full-time professional ministers tends to increase in prosperous Western churches, but is an unattainable goal in other parts of the world. Yet in the biblical narratives the notion of 'full-time professional church ministry' was the exception, not the rule. Besides this issue for pastors, there is also an incredible wealth of talent and calling in the pew; hopefully, we'll increasingly release and empower it for kingdom alignment and advancement. I think that a biblical understanding of vocation, calling, and work can enrich the church, especially in urban environments where we desire to see greater church multiplication."

BAM Affirmed

Meanwhile, the Business as Mission concept is increasingly understood and accepted in the Foursquare Church. Jonathan shares the example of a Foursquare pastor in a closed country who had tried to be a "full-time pastor," yet after being exposed to the BAM conversation, he reopened his small shoe repair shop and is amazed at how much more engaged he is with the neighborhood, with people asking for prayer when they stop by to have their shoes mended.

Since 2012, the Foursquare BAM Network has presented training at denominational conventions where they have had booths, given workshops, and networked with leaders. Jonathan shares, "There is a growing sense that 'BAM is a part of us.' The Foursquare Church family has innovation, flexibility, and creativity in its original and founding DNA. These values have and will serve us well as entrepreneurship and innovation are increasingly a necessity in this increasingly urban global reality."

BAM Curriculum at Bible College

Meanwhile, pastors, missionaries, and young entrepreneurs are also introduced to Business as Mission concepts at Life Pacific College, the Foursquare College in California with several hundred students from around the globe. Life Pacific used to focus on training for traditional pastoral roles yet is now expanding into other spheres. "We emphasize the importance of God's desire to transform and renew all areas: economic, social, and spiritual," explains Dr. Michael Bates, who developed a missional business administration degree at Life Pacific with the BAM worldview as a basis: "Not every student is entrepreneurially oriented and starts a business, but a kingdom mind-set is developed. We teach a holistic paradigm and encourage students to seek societal transformation to glorify God."

Sovereign River of God

Jonathan shares how BAM themes are becoming a part of conversations in global working groups—for example, in the discussion of urban strategies or how to serve refugee camps. "The impact of basic training in entrepreneurship can be significant in areas of poverty and displacement. While helping with basic necessities, why not also teach entrepreneurship from a Christian perspective?

"I see biblical BAM principles being helpful everywhere," concludes Jonathan. "I see this movement cutting across denominational lines. In wealthy environments or in slums, people are growing in these truths; and while they might not call it BAM, we can clearly see a sovereign river of God in our day and time."

PART II

BAM CONCEPT EXPLAINED

By Mats Tunehag

INTRODUCTION

By Mats Tunehag

Soviet Union, Rwanda, Indonesia, and Mats' Journey into BAM

Remember the Soviet Union? It was a communist country with a planned centralized economy, violations of human rights were prevalent, and it also lacked freedom to act in the marketplace. I was there and witnessed the dysfunctional state firsthand. It was like a giant statue with feet of clay, and it did eventually fall over and implode in December 1991.

One country became fifteen countries. One currency became fifteen currencies. One grand, artificial, and centrally planned economic system crumbled, and fifteen new nations had to regroup and try to adjust to a market-based global economy.

I kept traveling to the now former Soviet Union and kept working in Central Asia, in the "stans," such as Kazakhstan, Kyrgyzstan, Uzbekistan, and Tajikistan. But what I experienced there wasn't just geopolitical changes and turmoil. Many Christian agencies came to the region from all over the world, and I also witnessed quite a remarkable growth of people from a Muslim background becoming followers of Jesus.

Rampant Unemployment

At the same time, there was an exponential growth of unemployment and underemployment. It was on a scale that most of us find hard to fathom. With it came all kinds of social problems. How could we as followers of Jesus respond to this need? Businesspeople were needed. But churches and mission agencies did not call upon the people qualified to address these challenges.

So in the mid-1990s we started to explore how we could engage, equip, and connect Christians in business with the needs and opportunities in the Central Asia region. We started the Central Asia Business Consultation and ran it for ten years. The lessons learned— including developing processes and networks to listen, learn, share, and connect—were foundational for the later development of the global think tanks on Business as Mission.

Rwanda, Church Growth, and Genocide

A second game changer was the genocide in Rwanda in 1994. If our sole success criterion is church planting and growth, Rwanda was probably the ultimate success story in the history of church and missions. In about a hundred years, it went from 0 to approximately 90 percent of the population becoming members of various churches. But in the spring of 1994, about one million people were killed in just a few months. It literally was Christians killing Christians. Rwanda had people in church, but not church in people. The gospel had not transformed ethnic relations, politics, or media.

What Is Our Mission?

These tragic events forced me to review our mission. What is the mission of the church? How can we serve people and nations toward a holistic transformation, believing that God can transform individuals and communities, churches and nations? What does it mean to be a Christian in the marketplace? How can we do business as mission, law as mission, education as mission, and city planning as mission? How can we serve God and the common good? What does it mean in practice, and what are the lessons learned regarding seeking the *shalom* and prosperity of cities and nations as stated in Jeremiah 29? How do we affirm, equip, and deploy businesspeople to exercise their gifts of wealth creation for the nations as in Deuteronomy 8?

BAM x Three

BAM has three components: concept, praxis, and a movement. BAM is a biblical concept that is increasingly being applied around the world in many industries. The two global BAM think-tank processes, starting in 2002, have been instrumental in bringing about global cohesion and an increasing mutual understanding of the BAM concept.

But it is also a growing global movement of leaders in several constituencies: business, church, mission, and academia. The BAM Global Think Tanks have gathered intellectual and social capital: it has developed the BAM concept and a common language around it, as well as connected people and developed various networks. This has created an unprecedented connectedness of people and ideas.

BAM is certainly not a Western idea or network, and a large part of my journey into BAM has meandered through non-Western contexts.

BAM in Indonesia

Let me share a story from Indonesia, which illustrates the potential transformational power of business. It is part of my BAM journey. I witnessed firsthand how a Muslim village was transformed through prayer, Christian businesspeople, and owls. It was a warm and humid day in Indonesia. One may say almost too hot for a Swede. But the story that emerged was more than cool.

I spent a day with the mayor of a small Muslim village. We sat outside his house, drank tea, and nibbled on fruit, nuts, and sweets. He was enthusiastic and composed. As a devout Muslim, he had come to appreciate Christian businesspeople in a way that surprised him. There is a long and sometimes violent history of severe distrust and tension between Muslims and Christians in Indonesia.

The mayor told me that the village used to be quite poor. Rats ate 40 percent of the crops every year, and these creatures also spread disease. Collaboration for irrigation was nonexistent. There was a lack of entrepreneurial spirit, and it seemed that no one thought about praying for a difference.

Then one day, some Christian businesspeople visited the mayor and his village. They wanted to help, and they wanted to build bridges across a religious divide.

At first, the mayor declined. Why did businesspeople come and not charity workers or government people? On top of that, these people were Christians—not Muslims. But one Christian business-woman suggested that they could at least pray. She said that prayers make a difference; yes, God can make a difference. It was agreed. Something happened, and it became a turning point. The mayor invited them to come back and they did.

The team of Christian businesspeople did research and explored ways to kill the rats in an environmentally friendly way. They also researched how one could increase the agricultural production and start profitable businesses.

They found an owl called *Tyto alba* that eats rats but is also very hard to breed. Some told them it was impossible. But they prayed, conducted research, and it worked. I could see birdhouses every-where on the fields. Since then the loss of crops has decreased from 40 to 2 percent per year, and new wells and irrigation have doubled the annual yield of rice.

I asked the mayor why they didn't dig wells and develop irriga-tion before the businesspeople came. He said that the Christians changed their mind-set regarding work and working together, and they first and foremost taught them the importance of prayer, to always start with prayer. "Now we are open to change and we take action," said the mayor. "But we always start with prayer."

My Indonesian business friends have started business training courses in the village—based on biblical principles. They have also helped start small manufacturing businesses, improve marketing and sales, and strengthen local infrastructure.

This small village with 2,320 people has now become a model village in Indonesia. National television has portrayed it as a model on how to build bridges between Muslims and Christians, and as a model on how to develop transformational businesses. The village is also now a national learning center on how to breed owls that kill rats.

During my visit, I heard other testimonies on how concrete prayers had led to concrete answers—related to rain, a paved road, a job, a motorcycle, and more.

As we left the village, I was encouraged and felt privileged. I had witnessed significant indicators of economic, social, environmental, and spiritual transformation. I asked myself: What were some of the key contributing factors? Prayers, Christian businesspeople, and owls.

It has been an exciting journey, both surprising and overwhelming. But it is a true privilege to be a part of a global community that is on a *rediscovery* journey of biblical truths about work, justice, business, profit, and creating in community for community. We are witnessing a great *reawakening* in the church worldwide. May this lead to a *reformation*, as we shape and reshape our businesses for God and the common good.

David Skews (United Kingdom)
Being Globally Involved—"The Other Side of the Coin"

David Skews was successful as a shrewd, young businessman. Then unexpectedly, he lost everything. In the depths of his despair, he was challenged to start up a business again, but this time to do it totally differently: as a follower of Jesus. David took the challenge seriously, which set him on an adventurous journey: he witnessed a miracle-working God and worked with heads of state, while deciding to welcome problems "as old friends." David has become an experienced Business as Mission entrepreneur, and is nowadays involved with BAM globally (www.turnthecoin.com). "It all started from brokenness," says David.

"Look at the other side of the coin," said the pastor to David, while giving him a pound coin. These words were spoken over thirty years ago, on a dirty couch in a tiny, gloomy room in downtown Manchester, England. But these words had a profound and lasting impact. As a young, successful entrepreneur, David had thought the sky was the limit. He had enjoyed running his trading business in a "smart" way—getting good deals whenever and however, meanwhile pushing his staff to the limit and working even harder himself. His main aim was to get as much profit as possible. He seemed to reach his goals, but he failed to notice that his insatiable drive drove others away from him. So when bad times hit, he found out—to his surprise—that he hadn't made any real friends. Nobody wanted to lend him money to save his business. Even worse: girlfriend, staff, and friends abandoned him.

David looked at the pound in his hand and turned it around. On an impulse during a Sunday wander through the neighborhood, he had walked into a church but left before the service ended. The pastor had noticed David and felt an urge to find out about this young man; after hearing how David had lost everything, he went and visited him. As they were sitting and sharing in that dingy place, the Spirit of God gently entered the room, touching David's heart and mind. Although he had lost everything and felt utterly broken, hope came back. Slowly it dawned on David that a future might be possible again. Even owning a business. "Do it differently," the pastor insisted. "Look at the other side of the coin."

Converting the Business

God touched David, while challenging him to keep working with his business talents—but this time in a totally different way. Instead of seeking "to get," it meant learning to seek "to give." David started up a business in consultancy, advising businesses regarding safety issues in the workplace. He started up with nothing—even worse: with a debt of over 250,000 British pounds sterling, which he was determined to pay back, because he took God's challenge seriously. But what else did it mean? He didn't know. "I prayed that I needed someone to help me, since I didn't trust myself yet," shares David, while sitting in his garden in a quiet neighborhood in a town east of Liverpool. Looking back, there is so much to tell. "I wanted to be teachable and humble, but felt I needed to be held accountable." He had a connection with Alan, a leader of the church, who worked at a bank at the time. So when David started up his business, this was the first person he hired to work closely with him—with the intention to help him convert business practices. It led to earnest prayer while asking, "God, what does your kingdom look like in this situation? What is the 'other side of the coin'?"

"I needed to be held accountable."

It led David to a whole new level of trust in God, as the Resourcer of his business. Sometimes this went against his "common sense," as he was learning to listen and obey. David remembered the time when a VAT bill of five thousand pounds came in with only a few days to pay, while they hardly had anything in cash. "I sat down with Alan, and we asked God: 'What is the other side of the coin?' We felt challenged 'to give,' so we told our accountant to write a check of a hundred pounds and give it to someone in need." Instead of hoarding, worrying, and holding on, they learned about trust: letting go, looking up to God, and being generous. They were able to pay their bill on time. "We saw God at work, and this continually encouraged us to take the next step."

Another time, David had a profitable contract with a customer, but he wasn't at ease with it. "It was a contract to supply an arms company, but their values were awful. While attending their meeting to sign the contract the language among them was negative and aggressive. When I was in the alleyway with the contract in my hand, I wondered if God could be pleased with this and if I really should work with them. I turned around, walked back into the room, and gave the order back. I said to them that I didn't want to work with them. It made no logical sense, because we actually really needed the money. But by making this decision, I felt an inner release."

"We decided to welcome [trials] like old friends."

Although the growth of the new business was slow in the beginning, God sustained the business. Their "converted business" didn't go smoothly all the time. They tried listening to God but didn't always hear it right. They had hard times and made mistakes, but in these difficulties, they looked at "the other side of the coin." David says, "We greeted the trials we faced; we decided to welcome them like old friends. Trials can bring about greater joy and confidence, since discipline and courage are developed while walking through hard issues like customer services issues, lack of cash flow, or how to keep sales going."

Expecting Miracles

Yet in and through it all, by being serious about following God and acting in ways pleasing to him, their faith and expectancy grew that God would work on their behalf. "We expected miracles," says David.

One such miracle happened about ten years after he started the business. David was asked by an IT multinational, one of their clients, to share at their yearly award ceremony about the orphanage in Cambodia that David's company was supporting. "I warned them that it wouldn't be a nice story. I had been in Cambodia, and the needs of these children were horrendous. In this corporate setting, I described the suffering of the children and couldn't help crying. A lot of other people in the room were crying also. Afterward, the senior director overseeing global security came up to me and promised that our company would get a yearly order of two million dollars as long as we continued to serve the poor in Cambodia. That was an enormous amount for us, and this yearly order has sustained us over the years through a lot of difficulty."

Involved in Business as Mission

David's company supported endeavors like this orphanage, but this contract and the overall growth of the company brought their social involvement to another level. In 2005, their business set up a trust organization to channel finances and other recourses to help small businesses launch and become sustainable. Next to financing start-ups, they provided business advice—addressing legal, accountancy, sales, and marketing matters. Most of all, their goal is to encourage those businesses to operate on "the other side of the coin": to seek what they can *give* instead of what they can *get*. People started noticing, and as a result the government of an African country asked David to set up a school of entrepreneurship. David remembers walking and talking with the vice president about this idea. "We prayed together and I got a picture of a building and its surroundings, which I described. The president knew right away where the place was. The school became a reality, also thanks to the help of the multinational providing the building and the much needed IT."

Transforming Countries and Worldviews

In an Asian country, where foreign workers' lives aren't valued and are almost regarded as slaves, David and his company advised the government on safety issues. But next to convincing the government—even confronting some people—of the necessity to change rules, worldviews also needed transformation. Just providing safety waist belts to foreign workers wasn't enough, since many of them had fatalistic worldviews of God and life with a mind-set that thinks, "If we die, it is God's will." So David's company decided to approach the leadership of mosques, churches, and temples to join them in a "Value Life" campaign. Altogether the results were astounding: over a period of six years, the yearly death rate among foreign construction workers went down more than half: from 5.8 per 10,000 deathly casualties at work to 2.4.

David says, "That is 3,400 fatalities a year less; people who are still living. It is very rewarding to see such tangible results, but it was a struggle at the time. We were aware that we were touching difficult ground. Every meeting we went in, we asked for prayer coverage from our prayer team in the UK. It is a spiritual battle to be involved in changing worldviews and mind-sets."

Involved in BAM Globally

Meanwhile, David became involved with the global Business as Mission movement, as their trust organization would support small start-ups. "We didn't do very well in beginning," he says. "We would go over the plan and give money, but many of them just disappeared. We didn't have a good accountability system in place." But helping other start-ups was in various ways fruitful, such as lending money to a man who sold fruit on the roadside in a country in the northern part of Africa. The fruit seller needed 250 euros to buy a fruit cart to sell his melons on the town square. David heard about this through a missionary organization: "The fruit seller returned the 250 euros, even with interest. At first, they employed just two people, but now he has multiple shops and is one of the biggest fruit sellers in town. At that time he was a Muslim, but they are now known locally to be a Christian business."

David sold his business in 2014 and now solely focuses on supporting the BAM movement globally—through coaching owners of businesses around the world, speaking at and supporting BAM events, and through helping several mission agencies develop strategies to implement Business as Mission. "Mission agencies used to view BAM generally as a way to fund projects, but now I see a genuine seeking of what God is saying as they realize that BAM is about much more than raising finances and can truly help to bring transformation to the most challenging environments."

Gaps, Needs, and Opportunities

David sees a gap regarding BAM in and from Europe. "It is time for the Christian European business world to move," thinks David, who was mainly involved in Asia, but is redirecting his attention toward Europe to help develop BAM in that part of the world.

A need within BAM is for more professionals with a builder mind-set to become involved: "There are different kinds of business-people," he explains. "You have trader-types, as well as entrepreneurs who see and create opportunities. But there are also business-build-ers. We need more of those at this stage: professionals in finance, administration, HR, facilities, and marketing to help build businesses."

Wealth Creation

David is convinced that God wants to bless nations, and he wants us to be involved in blessing nations. "God gives us the ability to create wealth, *so we can bless others*. What Jesus taught us is not a prosperity message, because we don't bless others in order to receive a blessing; we certainly do not want to make deals with God! He sets the terms and conditions; we bless because it pleases God who already blessed us. It can be damaging when we focus on the blessing: profit is a reward for doing great business, not the sole focus. But profit is also needed; it is like oxygen to live for a business, but it is not the reason the business exists."

David learned about giving, to bless and be blessed. Thirty years ago, he started his journey with God from brokenness, but with expectancy and an eagerness to listen and learn: "My brain shifted from what I can *get* to what I can *give*. We tried in all areas of business to be followers of Jesus; we took prayer seriously and asked other people to pray for our business and involvements. We took words received through prophetic prayer seriously, by weighing and discussing what was communicated with us in prayer. We would do it, unless God told us not to do it. It has been an amazing journey. In my wildest dreams, I never thought to be involved with things like this."

CHAPTER 6

WEALTH CREATION

A Godly Gift and Command

By Mats Tunehag

As we do business, we create wealth—not only financial wealth but also social, cultural, intellectual, and spiritual wealth. The Bible talks about wealth in three ways: wealth creation, sharing, and hoarding. The last is condemned. Wealth sharing is encouraged and is often facilitated through NGOs and churches, but there is no wealth to be shared unless it has been created. As God has given us the ability to create wealth (Deut. 8:18), we need to recognize this to be a godly gift.

Let's look at the context of this statement in Deuteronomy 8. The people of Israel have been brought out of Egypt and are about to enter the Promised Land. God tells them what to expect and what to do. He explicitly states that there are good business prospects in mining and agriculture, and he admonishes them to pursue these opportunities. As a result, wealth will be created. But then a danger arises, or rather, two potential pitfalls.

First, God says there is a risk that people will think and say that they themselves have created wealth, failing to acknowledge the Lord in their success. This is what precedes verse 18. So God reminds them that he is the one who gives the gift and ability to create wealth. Thus wealth creation is a gift from God and he also commands us to engage in creating wealth.

Second, wealth creation is put into the context of the covenant. God entered into a covenant with Abraham and his descendants, blessing them so they could likewise bless others, locally and globally. But one could say blessings are beyond mere words. To bless others is to create all kinds of wealth and, in turn, share it. This is indeed a part of the covenant. And one mustn't forget God, the initiator of the covenant.

Wealth creation processes carried out through business should be mindful of both God and others. We should always have this dual goal: to do business for God *and* the common good. It makes a difference. Noah and his sons undertook a massive engineering project with this perspective, and it led to the salvation of humanity and creation. An equally impressive construction project was the Tower of Babel. God, however, was left out of this project; built on selfish motives, it led to the breakdown of society.

The gift and calling to create wealth is beyond a microfinance loan or a single small- or medium-sized business. It is about building nations and seeking the welfare of cities.

> This is what the Lord Almighty says to all those I carried into exile from Jerusalem to Babylon: Build houses and settle down; plant gardens and eat what they produce. Also, seek the peace and prosperity of the city. (Jer. 29)

In this verse from Jeremiah, we find the people of Israel in exile, in a country they didn't choose. But they mustn't sit and sulk, simply go into survival mode, or withdraw into religious ceremonies and meetings. No, they are commanded to start businesses, develop the local economy, and in doing so strive for *shalom*. *Shalom* is whole relationships filled with integrity. Similarly, business is about relationships with customers, clients, suppliers, staff, community, city officials, and environment. Seek *shalom* with all these partners and entities, as you seek to create wealth and prosperity for cities and nations.

In his encyclical letter *Laudato Si'*, Pope Francis writes: "Business is a noble vocation, directed to producing wealth and improving the world. It can be a fruitful source of prosperity for the area in which it operates, especially if it sees the creation of jobs as an essential part of its service to the common good."[1]

Or, as the Wealth Creation Manifesto puts it, "Wealth creation is a holy calling, and a God-given gift, which is commended in the Bible."[2]

Use it—for God and the common good.

---

1. *Encyclical Letter* Laudato Si' *of the Holy Father Francis on Care for Our Common Home* (May 24, 2015), #29.
2. See Appendix 1: Wealth Creation Manifesto.

Don Larson (Mozambique)

Building Food Factories in Developing Nations
to Bring Lasting Transformation

Don (middle) and his wife Terri (middle/
right) with Mozambican children.

Don Larson likes to take on huge challenges. This North American
moved to Mozambique to sink his teeth into establishing a just market
concept through a new business model in Africa. He is now on his
way: previously orphaned young men and women roast and pack-
age cashew nuts in his Sunshine Nut Company (https://sunshinenuts
.com)—with amazing, fresh-tasting nuts as a result. "Hope never
tasted so good," says Don.

Raw cashews are usually shipped to India or Vietnam, where
they are roasted and packaged weeks or even months later. "We
capture the freshness in country and put it in premium packaging,"
explains Don Larson. "Building local factories enables local roasting
and packaging, and allows the product to be fresh and crunchy—
creating a competitive advantage." Retail people, whose job it is to
buy nut products for large retail store chains, tell Don: "We never
knew what a fresh cashew nut tasted like."

The business is going well. In late 2014, Sunshine Nut Company first entered the US market. Within a few years' time, its products were sold in about three thousand retail stores, such as Ahold,

Whole Foods, Wegmans, and HEB. Sales in 2015 were nearly $1 million, the next year it doubled, and a year later $5 million in sales was expected. "We offer a premium quality brand," Don says. "Our price is competitive with the large nut companies, and we do great works with the profits of the company. It is a win-win scenario for all."

About forty people over the age of twenty have found employment at the Sunshine Nut factory, most of whom were recruited through job fairs at local orphanages where they grew up. Meanwhile, this factory also provides a need for a thousand people working at shelling factories in the northern part of Mozambique, while another fifty thousand cashew farming families receive a fair price for their crop to supply the factory.

Mozambique's Cashew Industry

In the 1970s, the nation of Mozambique was number one in cashew production and processing, until civil war and international banking policies decimated the industry. In recent years, many factories have started back up, but only 25 percent of Mozambique's cashews are shelled in-country, while farming communities are being exploited. Don: "I discovered farmers getting paid only a third to a fourth of what they should have been paid by outside traders, and I hear of many stories of intimidation. My aim is to strengthen the entire cashew value chain and grow the amount of shelling done in-county."

Unsettling Conversation

Don's search for the way to transform the lives of the poor for the long term started after an unsettling conversation at a Ghanaian airport in 2004. He had been working as an executive for Hershey's for some time, where he had brought innovation and opportunity within different areas of the company. As a result, Don was asked to do so again as director of cocoa operations and traveled to Ghana to assess the cocoa crop. On returning home, what began as an amiable conversation with some college graduates turned hostile when they realized Don was one of the largest cocoa buyers in the world. They accused him of being part of the problem of poverty because of the low price Hershey was paying to farmers. Don—blown away by the level of poverty he had just encountered—had presumed he was part of the solution, since he was buying local products and thereby providing income for millions. In his mind, it was the market—the law of supply and demand—that dictated prices. During this conversation, the students defended fair trade, but Don saw weaknesses there: "Artificially raising prices often creates imbalances in supply, which can lead to prices tumbling down for lack of demand. Fair trade is an option on a small scale for people willing to support the movement." The conversation became even more unsettling for him, as Don realized that a business model to eradicate poverty didn't exist.

Back in the States, life seemed to continue as usual. But in the following years, his success and career began to feel empty. Then, in 2008, during a five-month sabbatical, he went on a spiritual journey. He had been living a normal and appropriate Christian lifestyle—going to church, attending Bible studies and Promise Keeper conferences—but he always felt as if he was on the sideline, sitting on the fence.

During this spiritual journey he sought solitude, and while at an Oceanside Beach hotel during winter, he recorded his decision: "God, I totally surrender. I fully commit to you and give you the second half of my life. Use me, completely." Don remembers: "I felt as if God was entering that room, as if I could reach behind me and touch him."

Jumping Off the Fence

Don expected he would go to seminary and get involved with traditional missions, but God had a plan that better suited his personality, gifts, and experiences. He had said goodbye to the food industry, so it was a surprise to him when an idea popped into his head: "Build food factories in third world nations to bring lasting economic transformation." He didn't know what that would look like, but he felt as if he had finally jumped off that fence and was about to enter the playing field, into the place for which he was destined.

Partnering with God

As Don pondered the idea over the next months, he focused on the question of how *God* would run a company. While seeking, praying, and receiving prophetic words, Don felt the concept evolve.

The factories would provide first-class food, give away the majority of the profits, and help both orphans and local farming families. Don: "This business model was to be built on a 90 percent distribution of the company's net proceeds back to the poor and orphaned in Africa. The food processing factories would process the harvests from small farm holders in Africa, building the factories near farming communities to help bring the farmers a market while paying them fairly. Meanwhile the world-class food factories would help teach food processing courses at the local universities to multiply opportunity. It was to be called the Sunshine Approach."

Don birthed this business concept, as it were, in this material world, but he did so in close partnership with the Triune God: Father, Son, and Holy Spirit. The concept birthed out of this partnership is dear and sacred to Don, especially the 90 percent giving away of the net profit, which is a nonnegotiable. Don wrote this down on paper and signed it. He knew beforehand that it would be a huge challenge, but he wanted to seal his commitment and determination: the essentials could never be changed. Don is convinced that if he is faithful, then God will be faithful and somehow back him up.

Allocation of Profit

The business plan is becoming a reality in Mozambique, where they produce the best possible nuts and are involved with orphans. Don's wife, Terri, has a background in education and is responsible for the Sunshine Approach Foundation. She allocates the proceeds of two-thirds of the 90 percent net profit; a third goes to projects in the communities to raise the standard of living, while another third goes to orphan care. One example is building homes for widows and matching them with orphans so the kids can grow up in a family-type setting, meanwhile helping to build local community and family life in this way.

"Some of these orphan kids have become like our own kids," says Don, "which is very rewarding. Our factory hires young adults from the orphanages, because we want to further educate them, and whenever possible promote them into positions of leadership. One of them, Binario, is a very smart and eager young man. We hired him three years ago, and he is now running the place."

With the other 30 percent of the profit, Don wants to further extend the business concept: "In other African nations we also want to build food factories, either nut factories or other types of crops grown by small farmers—because we want to spread the prosperity resulting from this type of business model."

Influential

While export and sales revenues are growing, influential organizations are taking notice of both Don's business model and his faith. In 2016, Don won the silver medal at the International Peace Award, held in Rio de Janeiro. He was second out of seventeen chosen CEOs globally. "While Terri and I were toured around in Rio, a top UN official confided: 'Our understanding is that religion causes problems, but we hardly grasp that religion and business can bring peace and wealth; we need to learn in this area.'" Don is regularly asked to present the Sunshine Approach at influential institutions, such as the World Economic Forum, Grow Africa, Oxford Business School, and the European Economic Summit. He has also been asked to become a panel member of the Nobel Prize Forum.

Adventure

This "God assignment" fits Don's personality and work experience. In his former jobs, he was "a turnaround guy," knowing a lot about much. He was the lead negotiator at Hershey's—in titles such as director of global sourcing or cocoa operations. In these roles, he often needed to negotiate and fight for a breakthrough. Such traits have proven to be invaluable in this present endeavor, as he has to circumnavigate delicate and difficult interactions with governments, suppliers, retailers, and nationals.

Regarding his personality, Don acknowledges: "I loved the adrenaline rush of my former sport cars, motorcycles, air balloon, and general fast life. But life over here in Africa gives me my portion also. I joke that I can take 'being held at gunpoint' off my bucket list, which happened when we were being robbed of our car. Every day is an adventure over here."

It might suit Don's personality, but it is certainly an adventure different from driving a fast sports car—even though fast driving and life in Mozambique are equally dangerous. For example, when a local witch doctor puts a spell on someone's life, Don shares, "My wife is battling for the life of an orphan. He was cursed and now has a wound that won't heal. Such things are very real over here in Africa. Terri is fighting for his life; she has been battling already for months with medication and through prayer."

In general, the Larsons have experienced an overall heavy spiritual atmosphere: for no apparent reason, couples who came to visit started fighting in their marriage, and Don and Terri quickly learned they needed to be watchful themselves. The spiritual realm has become a reality to take into account.

Preparation

Becoming more acquainted with a spiritual reality was also part of their preparation time—from the moment Don decided to give the second part of his life to God until they arrived in Mozambique. During those eighteen months, they became familiar with the supernatural in new and various ways, often through prophetic words from people who didn't know anything about them. "At a conference," Don recalls, "a lady came up to us who told us that we would know things partially within three weeks, and within three months we would know what to do in detail." Three weeks later, the idea popped in his head about building factories, while he shared in detail how it became clear that Mozambique was the place to build nut factories. That was exactly three months to the date. "It is a God thing," Don says. "I learned to step out, even in cases when I wasn't sure I had heard right. But every time I did, it turned out to be good. I'm not perfect and I'm still learning, but I think God is most of all interested in our obedience."

Life definitely changed for the Larson family after Don decided to give the second part of his life to God, but they don't have any regrets. "We do not have an abundance in material things anymore; our easy life and our toys are gone. But life is most exciting when you are doing and living your purpose; in my case, that is pioneering and demonstrating a new business model. It is about knowing him intimately, knowing ourselves, and finding our unique assignment. That is so fulfilling and meaningful."

CHAPTER 7

GOD RESTORES THE MARKETPLACE

By Mats Tunehag

The prospects were not good. In fact, they were really bad, even disastrous. The city was under siege, and everything pointed toward a defeat. People would be assaulted, hurt, and killed; houses would be burned down, and the remaining citizens of Jerusalem would be deported to a foreign land.

In this doomsday context, God told the prophet Jeremiah to make an investment—in the doomed city! Sounds like bad advice, buying property in a besieged area during a war. But it was supposed to be a prophetic action by doing real business.

Jeremiah conveyed the message loud and clear: God will restore his people and the city, and the signs of a restored nation would be found in a functioning marketplace.

Jeremiah buys a field from a relative, using his birthright. The payment is fair and conducted in front of witnesses. Deeds are issued and kept for posterity. This, however, is a prophetic purchase: "For this is what the Lord Almighty, the God of Israel, says: Houses, fields and vineyards will again be bought in this land" (Jer. 32:15). After war, destruction, despair, and exile, restoration will come, and it will come from God. The indicators of the restoration are seen in marketplace functions.

Jeremiah performed a prophetic act when he purchased the land. It involved a financial transaction, title deeds and archives, and a long-term investment with a potential return many years down the road. These are all present and future indicators of a God-approved economy. These are signs of a transformed society, of justice in the marketplace. The wider context in Jeremiah talks about benefits from building businesses and growing the economy; wealth is created, there is joy, and there are festivities and gratitude to God:

> The restored people would have lives of work, enjoyment, feasting, and worship all tied into one. The picture of planting, harvesting, playing music, dancing and enjoying the harvest depicts the pleasure of work in faithfulness to God.[1]

Jeremiah 32 shows that God wants business and businesses that grow. A God-inspired nation has a legal and societal framework conducive for business development. Let me list a few things that are implied or explicitly mentioned in this biblical narrative, all part of a marketplace for peace and prosperity:

- A Rule of Law society
- Birth certificates (some kind of officially recognized identity)
- Property laws
- An established currency
- A functional system for economic transactions
- Honesty and transparency in business dealings
- Title deeds, records, and archives
- Buying and selling works
- Return on investment and long-term thinking

Other lessons we can learn:
- There was a willingness to take risks
- The importance of acknowledging God and honoring the covenant in business
- Readiness to follow God's instruction and take steps of faith
- Rejoice in the harvest/profit
- Work and worship were integrated
- Wealth was created and prosperity came to the city

---

1. "Jeremiah & Lamentations and Work," *Theology of Work Bible Commentary*, ed. Will Messenger (Peabody, MA: Hendrickson Publishers, 2016), 469.

We see a God here who is engaged in the marketplace. It is part of God's mission in the world and throughout history. The events in Jerusalem with Jeremiah show God at work in history. Business as Mission, BAM, is also a part of that story—his story.

As David Green, founder of Hobby Lobby, puts it, "There is a God, and He's not averse to business. He's not just a 'Sunday Deity.' He understands margins and spreadsheets, competition and profits."[2] Lastly, "It is good to manage even our worldly affairs in faith, and to do common business with an eye to the providence and promise of God."[3]

---

2. David Green, *More Than a Hobby: How a $600 Startup Became America's Home and Craft Superstore* (Nashville: Thomas Nelson, 2005).

3. Matthew Henry (1662–1714), in a comment on Jeremiah 32, vol. 4, *Matthew Henry's Commentary on the Whole Bible* (Peabody, MA: Hendrickson, 2009).

Achim (Central Asia)

Business: A Natural Way to Share, Show, and Disciple

Local couple who received a loan to develop their land to
grow cotton. (Photo courtesy of the ones interviewed)

*Business is the most natural way to relate to non-Christians, to live out
your faith, and to disciple people. This is Achim's strong conviction. He
speaks from twenty years of experience, both in traditional missions
and in a Business as Mission setting.*

In his late twenties, Achim[4] moved with his wife to a majority
Muslim country in Central Asia. In this cross-cultural context, this
Western European couple learned the local language and raised their
children, with the aim to be a blessing to the people to whom they
felt called. Sent by their church to do charitable work and plant a
church, they later developed a microfinance business.

Business

"Through our business we want to provide high quality financial
services for the long-term development of the country," says Achim.
They offer small loans and service the small enterprise sector, helping locals to set up small businesses with one to ten employees. They

---

4. Names, country, and company have been changed or are unspecified for
security reasons. Photo courtesy of the ones interviewed.

also provide loans for mortgages to build houses, and for medical care and education. They have built a solid reputation in their region during the fifteen years they have been in business so far. Achim: "We protect our clients. We don't want them to get trapped in debt, and we therefore sometimes advise them to save instead of taking a loan. We also check if they have loans elsewhere, and usually don't give a second or third loan. Because of that, we have lost some good clients, but people have come to understand that we are concerned about them and have built a reputation of trustworthiness."

Achim and his wife came to plant churches and believe in the Business as Mission concept, but they don't see themselves as "missionaries." "Muslims consider missionaries to be what we would call 'terrorists'; namely, being paid to change the religion and culture of the people with force. The word *missionary* is not in the Bible either," continues Achim. "What was Paul called, and what did he do? He was called apostle and started a tent-making business. Before he made tents, he was mistrusted and thrown out within weeks. I think this happened because he was not working long and close enough with the local people to disciple believers and appoint elders."

Building Relationships in a Natural Way

The couple is positive about the holistic approach of the BAM concept, since owning a business is—at least, in their cultural context—more genuine, natural, and effective in order to build healthy relationships. A business provides opportunities to build good relations with employees, clients, and colleagues in the local business world. Achim has sixty employees, almost all of them Muslims. "It is common knowledge that most friendships develop while at work," says Achim. "In Genesis 1 we read that God worked, and he told us to go and work. It is part of how he made us. Through working together, we can relate easily and naturally."

"Through working together, we can relate easily and naturally."

Good relationships are key when listening to each other while exchanging experiences, ideas, and beliefs. This is true everywhere, but even more so in this particular Asian country, where it is dangerous to talk about important things over the phone, let alone in public places. With their oppressive Soviet past, the locals still fear that "the KGB might listen." Achim: "Sometimes I hear Christians having discussions about Jesus in the marketplace, but they are not taken seriously by the local people, since matters of importance aren't discussed publicly." Achim, his wife, and their grown children are invited into peoples' homes, where mutual sharing takes place: intimate and private subjects but also business, politics, faith, and God. "That's what friends discuss."

"When money gets involved, you tend to go to a much deeper level with people."

Building relationships with friends, but also with clients, can be more natural and genuine as a business owner. This is especially so in Achim's case of providing loans. "We connect with our clients through something they really need. We sell services, advice, and loans. They are ready to pay, and a real deal is happening. How we work with money shows what we think, what we value, and who we are. When money gets involved, you tend to go to a much deeper level with people. We see this with clients, but also with our employees: how much salary we pay, and if we decide to give a bonus or not. These are all deep issues, and they go to the core of people's hearts."

"Stop Being Nice"

Achim's experience is that within missionary circles, the general assumption is to be as nice as possible: "Missionaries attract, befriend, and serve people, in the hope for an opportunity to tell them the gospel. You give them what they think they need, so that afterward you can give them what you think they need. You always try to be nice and give."

Achim's personality comes across as gentle, friendly, and patient, but as a business owner he needed to become "less nice." For example, he learned to become sterner in confronting people, such as the neighbors who were hanging laundry illegally from the balconies of their office building: "I'd say something about it, but nothing would change. Finally my board members told me, 'Achim, this is a bank building; laundry can't be hanging out here. You think it's okay, but it's not.' They told me I needed 'to stop being a missionary and become less nice.' It meant being more disciplined, first of all in my own life. To do what I promised, not accept any excuses from myself for not doing my job, and to expect the same from others. It's about being accountable and expecting others to be accountable."

Accountability

Through the type of business—lending money—Achim and his employees need to keep their clients accountable. As a business owner, he also needs to do so in his daily work with employees: "If someone is not doing a good job, I need to correct him, give an oral or written warning, and if nothing helps I need to be willing to fire the person."

"God holds us accountable," he continues. "We will stand before him one day, and he will hold us accountable for what we have done with our lives. The parable of the talents in Matthew 25 teaches us to be responsible and productive. We don't have to double what has been entrusted to us, but God is at least expecting some interest."

Good Resolutions but No Accountability

In a church, charity, or mission setting, we can be soft, but sometimes too soft. Achim: "We do Bible study, hear good things, and make resolutions to change things in our lives, but we're not yet out the door and have already forgotten our resolutions. In a business setting, where we work together on a daily basis, it can be easier to keep each other accountable. As Christians we need to be intentional about such things and take time to think through biblical values and how that applies in daily life and work."

"He loved praying with me but didn't want to obey the word."

What Achim learned about accountability in his business setting, he started to apply to his church setting. For several years, he prayed and read the Bible with someone who was leading worship in his local church in Central Asia. Then Achim started to keep him accountable. "As it turned out, he loved praying with me but didn't want to obey the word. When I realized this, I reminded him many times that to love God means obeying his commandments.

He was not listening, so eventually I stopped meeting him. Many Christians are unproductive, but few are held accountable. Only when we address issues and have healthy conflicts do we get quality in relationships, ministry, and work, because we bother enough to address issues and real love can flow from there. Then people will say that these guys are different. They love each other."

Pre-decision Discipleship

Business offers some unique opportunities for "pre-decision discipleship"—helping people of other faiths to get acquainted with gospel values and then start living them out themselves. One of those gospel values is generosity.

Achim: "In our country people are generally quite stingy. They give little. Over the years, our employees have witnessed that we care for our workers and other poor and that we are generous toward them and help them when they are in trouble. Our watchman also works as a welder. In an accident, he broke his legs in several places and the operation didn't go well. For months he suffered, and we decided to take him to a hospital in the capital to do the operation again. We paid for it, but we learned to our pleasant surprise that our other workers also wanted to contribute. They offered themselves willingly; they had learned the joy of giving."

When a business helps their workers or gives aid to the community, it is much different from aid given by a charity. Achim explains, "Our workers see that we as a business support the community because we want to. They see us doing it, and they follow. It is different when they receive help from charities. When we as a business give to the poor, the people are thankful. But when charities give to the poor, they aren't thankful, because they expect it from them. In their eyes, 'it is the job of the charities to give.' These charities are part of the system 'as givers,' like the people partake of the system 'as receivers.' This system won't challenge them to start giving themselves. But people don't expect a business to help since we don't have the obligation to give, and somehow that sets an example they want to follow."

"We think we have the main thing, but we have narrowed the gospel and thereby completely missed the point."

The Gospel Message Takes Place in Real Life

The gospel message is meant to be lived out in the here and now, through applying values such as accountability and generosity, where we live and work. For many decades, the main paradigm within many church denominations has been, "You need to get saved so you can have eternal life." The gospel message gives indeed eternal hope, but it is also meant to bring justice, peace, and hope in the here and now. Achim: "We think we have the main thing, but we have narrowed the gospel and thereby completely missed the point. Remember Rwanda? This country had 90 percent Christians, and the people went to church. But the gospel message wasn't in the people. People started killing each other in the millions. What went wrong? A better example is a missionary who traveled in Brazil and felt God guiding him to a small village. He found out that the people would benefit greatly from an automatic coffee harvester. He worked for many years to invent and develop it, the first fully automatic coffee harvester in the world. Nowadays when you enter that area, you sense a bit of heaven: it's clean and neat; the people are working and are taking care of the poor among them. This story amplifies that the gospel message takes place in real life, it happens in our communities. The church is meant to encourage this, like Jesus said, 'Go!' We are meant to make the gospel tangible in the communities where we work and live."

Love, Hope, and Faith

For Achim and his family, their "adopted" community has become their home over the past twenty years. Although his children are grown now and study in Western Europe, they pleaded with their parents to never sell their home in the country they grew up in. They shouldn't worry, however, since Achim and his wife have plans to stay. They are enjoying their close-knit community, where they have strong friendships with both local Muslims and other expatriates. "We love the people of our community," says Achim. "They in turn esteem us a lot. We can also bring hope, through providing jobs and work. This is important in an area where there is hardly any hope for a better life."

Love, hope, and faith—these are what they aim to bring, but what they also need for themselves. Through their business they benefit the country, but they have dreams to do more in the future, especially by helping to develop small businesses. A striving sector of small and medium businesses can greatly benefit a country. "We need faith, also in business," says Achim. "We often think too small; we have a vision to grow the business into new levels of influence. But business is also about risk-taking and that is 'having faith' in biblical language."

CHAPTER 8

BUSINESS AS MISSION

A Biblical Perspective

By Mats Tunehag

Although Business as Mission, BAM, is a relatively new term (in English), it is based on biblical concepts. Other expressions often used include "transformational business," "missional business," "business for transformation," "great commission companies," and "kingdom business." The BAM concept is holistic in nature, believing that God has the power to transform people and communities, spiritually, economically, socially, and environmentally—in and through business. Thus we believe that God calls, equips, and deploys people to serve him and the common good in the marketplace.

BAM is a part of a wider global movement, recognizing and responding to God's call to take the whole gospel to the whole person in the whole world. The applications of BAM, however, may vary from time to time, from country to country, and from business to business.

BAM Is a Paradigm

The dichotomy (the divide) between sacred and secular, between spiritual and physical realms, stems from Greek Gnostic philosophy. Although this nonbiblical binary approach has been deemed by the church to be a heresy, it still permeates our thinking, our theology, and our mission strategy.

This has also resulted in a flawed view of the church and its members—as "the pyramid of Christ" instead of the biblical concept of the body of Christ. We tend to encourage climbing the pyramid, where "serving God full time" reaches its climax at the top. This nonbiblical view is common and influences most churches on all continents. The Greek Gnostic way of thinking values people with "spiritual vocations" and looks down on people dealing with business. To be a pastor is often seen as a higher calling or a spiritual ministry. We even use the term "full-time ministry." So, if one really wants to serve God, one should aim at climbing the pyramid, toward the "higher callings." Thus businesspeople are often viewed as not serving God but rather dealing with mammon.

The collective body of Christ suffers from this self-imposed dichotomy made between clerical and lay ministries. Sometimes, Christians denigrate or unwittingly hold an unfavorable opinion of those with secular jobs. They tend to vouchsafe approval to those associated with business if they give their money to spiritual works through the church or a mission agency. But just as God calls and equips people to be Bible translators or evangelists, he also calls and equips people to do business in order to serve him and others.

Business as Mission recognizes the body of Christ. We need to tear down the "pyramid of Christ" that permeates so much of our thinking, language, and actions. If God has called you to business, don't lower yourself to become a pastor! If you are called to business, then that is your highest calling—and likewise, if you are called to be a pastor. We are all given unique gifts and strengths to apply toward spreading the kingdom of God. There is no pyramid to climb, but there is a world to serve!

BAM Is Rooted in Scripture

God is the original Entrepreneur, who created an infinite number of good things, and we are created in God's image to be creative and to create good things as well. God told Adam and Eve to "till the garden," thus to be involved in a value-adding process. Business is rooted in God's character and in whom we are created to be.

As stated in the Wealth Creation Manifesto: "Wealth creation is rooted in God the Creator, who created a world that flourishes with abundance and diversity. We are created in God's image, to co-create with Him and for Him, to create products and services for the common good."[1]

---

1. See Appendix 1: Wealth Creation Manifesto.

The central business activity of providing meaningful and sustainable employment is a demonstration of justice and love, grounded in the character of God. In history, there are many examples of God-fearing men and women who have loved God and served people through business. Abraham was a successful businessman, Jesus worked in a small family business for many years, and the honorable woman in Proverbs 31 operated her own business.

Although unemployment is a consequence of the fall, it is not a sin to be unemployed. Unemployment, however, denies a person to be what God has intended for all of us to be: creative and able to support ourselves and others. Providing jobs with dignity is a righteous action; it is, in fact, helping people to grow in the image of God.

Through Jesus Christ, God restores creation, including work and creativity. We are called to play a role in God's restoration process by helping to restore the inherent dignity and value of work. Work is something that is simultaneously *deeply divine* and *deeply human*. As God took pleasure in the physical aspect of his creation, we too can delight in creating useful and excellent products and services.

BAM Is Being a Follower of Jesus

What does Jesus declare as a key characteristic of his true followers? Helping the hungry, the thirsty, the naked, the sick, and those in prison (Matt. 25). What is a major underlying cause of malnourishment, starvation, homelessness, disease, and limited access to medical treatment, as well as debt and crime? Unemployment! Providing people with jobs alleviates and prevents these dire conditions. One may paraphrase Jesus' words in Matthew 25: "I was jobless and you gave me a job!"

Jesus' ministry is clearly one of both preaching and demonstrating God's kingdom (Isa. 58:6–7; Luke 7:22). Most people who came to Jesus had emotional, physical, and social needs, and Jesus constantly and consistently met such needs. Nicodemus, an intellectual who had "spiritual" questions, was an exception, not the rule. Notably, Jesus never turned away from those who came to him in need. There was no wrong or unworthy need, problem, or question.

Jesus stated that healing the sick, feeding the hungry, caring for the grieving, and so on, are manifestations of God's kingdom.

He even taught us to pray, "Your kingdom come." *BAM is about being an answer to Christ's prayer*—in and through business—so that physical, social, emotional, economical, and spiritual needs may be addressed and met.

What is "good news" to the unemployed? We mustn't try to be "more spiritual" than Jesus; he spent the bulk of his ministry meeting needs in the "secular" realm. He never apologized for spending so much time and effort dealing with ordinary human needs.

Courtney Rountree Mills (Kenya)

*Training Entrepreneurs to Integrate Faith
with Work and Grow Their Business*

Courtney (left) talking with one of Sinapis's alumni, Frank
Omondi, managing director of Ten Senses Africa, a
fair trade macadamia and cashew producer. (Photo
courtesy of Karibu Nyaggah, cofounder, Sinapis)

*In Kenya, 85 percent of the population confesses to be Christian, yet
this African country is among the most corrupt in the world and
struggles with 40 percent unemployment. Courtney Rountree Mills
is convinced that Christian entrepreneurs are the key to catalyzing
change. But there is a problem: they perceive faith and work as two
different worlds. To help them integrate the two, Courtney started
Sinapis (www.sinapis.org) with the mission of training young entrepreneurs to alleviate financial and leadership poverty.*

In 2009, as a young American student, Courtney Rountree Mills
traveled to Kenya for the first time to research bottlenecks for economic growth in East Africa. This research was part of her study for
a graduate degree in political and economic development at Harvard University's Kennedy School. While in Kenya, she saw much
economic potential: a strong work ethic, a growing middle class of
young professionals, and some large African-based companies that
were creating innovative market models and scaling rapidly. While
money and help seemed available for large and middle-sized com-

panies, eager young entrepreneurs with business ideas were left out in the cold. She identified this as a major bottleneck that she wanted to tackle in her calling to fight poverty. As a result, Courtney and her cofounders returned to Nairobi a year later to launch Sinapis with the aim of accelerating business start-ups by providing rigorous, highly practical business training, as well as help in finding access to funding.

Integration Issue

During her research, she came across another problem. When she decided to buy a car in order to get around easier in Kenya, a friend warned her, "If someone tells you he is a born-again Christian, don't buy a car from him. He is almost certainly a con artist." At first Courtney thought he was joking, but when she wanted the engine checked at the dealership, the salesman responded, "Oh, no, no. You don't have to do that! I'm a born-again Christian!" When it turned out that the car was no good, she realized the extent of the problem. "People in the marketplace were prostituting Jesus' name for economic gain. To be a Christian had a negative connotation, one equal to being called a fraud."

> *"Life on Sunday and life on Monday are as different as life on Mars and Venus."*

The problem runs deep in Kenya, since followers of Christ are rarely taught how to be disciples in their daily working lives. As a result, they are ill-equipped to live out Christian values and ethics in the marketplace. "Nearly all Kenyans know about Jesus," says Courtney. "They can quote Scripture better than I can. But there is an integration issue. Life on Sunday and life on Monday are as different as life on Mars and Venus."

Tackle Two Issues at the Same Time

Courtney knew that a lack of integrity in leadership, such as corruption in government, is related to economic stagnation. She was developing training for entrepreneurs so they could start businesses, create jobs, and help alleviate poverty. But how should she tackle the leadership problem? That seemed like a different issue altogether. But then it dawned on Courtney that successful business leaders have an enormous influence on society. Be it for good or bad. "Entrepreneurs are admired like celebrities," Courtney remarks, "and even entrepreneurs at the lowest levels are often the community movers and shakers." If Sinapis could empower entrepreneurs to grow their businesses and use their influence to fight corruption and injustice in their societies, then Sinapis could tackle both issues simultaneously.

Courtney knew it was not in her power to change Kenya's corrupt political system, but she could start from the bottom-up by training future leaders. With a long-term vision, young entrepreneurs could become powerful influencers and inspiring examples of Christlike leadership in their communities.

Integrated Way of Learning

Completing the six-month Sinapis course is no small accomplishment. It asks twenty hours a week of the participant, applying what has been learned during the Saturday classes in the entrepreneur's business throughout the week. Because of this integrated way of learning, only Kenyans who are owners or CEOs of businesses are accepted. "They get field work assignments to complete during the week," explains Courtney, "which are related to the topics discussed on Saturdays. The following week they discuss with each other what they applied during the week. It is a powerful way to learn through both experience and mutual support."

The Economic Gain of Trustworthiness

"Take the theme of trustworthiness," continues Courtney. "We explain how political corruption is undermining economic growth, how the lack of trustworthiness is the cause for sky-high interest rates—even up to 30 percent, since many don't pay their loans back. The lack of trust is also causing all kinds of inefficiencies, like the tendency to double-check everything, which is costing the economy much time and money."

To bring such issues close to home, the participants of the training are asked to calculate how much time they spend weekly on visiting their suppliers to make sure they receive the needed product, as well as the time spent in preparing for plan B or C in case the product isn't delivered. "At first they get very angry when they realize the extent of the problem," shares Courtney. "They want change, and we help them see how they can do it. We explain that they can increase the spiritual capital in the country. Every time they deliver on time—even when it costs them to keep a promise—they deposit trust in a spiritual bank account. Every time they don't, they deduct trust. But eventually, when their clients start to realize that they are dependable, they will tell others. They know from experience: when you find a trustworthy supplier in Kenya who delivers products on time, it is like you have found gold."

Training in Cooperation with Churches

In 2011, the first Sinapis course was launched. It was hard work to recruit the first students, but word about the quality of the program quickly spread. Five years later, over six hundred entrepreneurs have been accelerated with now well over two hundred entrepreneurs a year trained. Sinapis has grown to over thirty staff and trainers and provides training in classes ranging from twenty-five to forty students each throughout the year in three cities in Kenya.

There is the benefit of an economic ecosystem within the church. "The church in Africa is where community happens. . . . Here you can find . . . aspiring entrepreneurs, mentors, and professional experts, as well as suppliers and customers."

Sinapis partners mostly with churches. Even though the church and business worlds can seem to be miles apart, Courtney saw the benefit in working closely together. Kenya's large church culture has the potential to influence marketplace values, and there is the benefit of an economic ecosystem within the church. "The church in Africa is where community happens," Courtney says. "Here values are instilled, and here you can find in one place aspiring entrepreneurs, mentors, and professional experts, as well as suppliers and customers."

Geared toward the Kenyan Culture

Sinapis is growing fast within Kenya and expanding to other countries. But in each country, Courtney expects the training will have different focal points. She learned through experience that business knowledge alone is not enough; it is also important to identify cultural mind-sets and spiritual strongholds that hinder development. In Kenya, one such mind-set is the tendency for people to hold on to property with all their might once they own it. At first she didn't understand why successful and intelligent Kenyans would start behaving unprofessionally when an investor would offer a hundred thousand dollars in exchange for a share in the company. "I would tell our students, 'Take it, take it, take it!' but I saw investors go home frustrated. Then we discovered that there are issues stemming from colonial times. Kenya became independent in the sixties, and up to that time, Kenyans weren't allowed to own anything. As a result, they cling with an iron fist to ownership. They are either the sole owner, or have their mother or brother as co-owner. Their fear of letting go of control can make them unreasonable in negotiation and keep their businesses forever tiny. We realized that mind-set needed attention."

As a result, Sinapis put extra emphasis on teaching biblical stewardship: the idea that God is the owner of your company, and you are the steward of it. Therefore, you should manage it in line with his heart. At the same time, the curriculum also shares stories of successful companies around the world and how they grew through partnering with others—either by offering a part of the company to investors or to professionals with needed expertise.

Long-Term Mind-Set

Another common cultural mind-set hindering successful business growth is short-term thinking. Courtney says, "Kenyans tend to start a small business to earn a bit of extra money on the side, or to be able to pay for the school tuition of their kids. In business, they tend to copycat or underprice others, and don't put a lot of effort into innovation, excellence, or delivering on promises."

Participants in Sinapis start to develop a vision for the long-term when challenged by companies such as Sony, a beloved brand in Kenya. "Sony developed a vision in the forties to change how the world thought about Japanese quality," explains Courtney, "which wasn't good at the time. But Sony had a fifty-year vision to change this, and eventually changed the world's public opinion about a whole country to the extent that now people think of many Japanese products as extremely high quality. The greatest companies are long-term thinkers and are transforming culture."

Fast-Track Program

The impact of the Sinapis training is researched and evaluated in an annual alumni survey, which found that 77 percent of entrepreneurs experience a totally changed mind-set in terms of relating faith to their business. During the training program, trainers see people quitting their other jobs to start pouring themselves into their own business wholeheartedly. They start to think about consumer needs and which products could advance the country, while developing greater vision to become influencers in the marketplace and society. "We empower our entrepreneurs to live out their Christian values," says Courtney. "What being a Christian means in the marketplace, and how they can make a difference in society. For example, one of our entrepreneurs started soccer events to bring together tribes before an election year to promote peace. Another started an entrepreneurship program in prisons to help prisoners create an economic path for themselves after they get out, while other entrepreneurs have funded churches in the slums."

"We empower our entrepreneurs to live out their Christian values."

"Grand ideas are described in business plans like 'In fifty years' time, we want Kenya to be known for integrity in business,'" Courtney says with a smile. At the end of the training there is a competition: A handful of Sinapis's top students enter a 'Fast Track Fellows' program with six months of intensive extra coaching and assistance in finding investors. They also are given the opportunity to compete for $10,000 to invest in their business by pitching their ideas to investors in Sinapis's annual business plan competition.

Gideon's Story

Gideon in front of the new school building. (Photo courtesy
of Jeanne Rohrs, communication manager, Sinapis)

Courtney has witnessed firsthand the incredible potential of
Kenyans. One story close to her heart is the story of Gideon. Gideon
really struggled in school and needed fourteen years to get through
the eighth-grade levels required in Kenya. Then, in 2008, Gideon
became burdened by the need in his community for early childhood education. Thinking back about his own experience, he was
convinced that all children, not just gifted students, can learn to
thrive. Despite having no formal training in education, he trusted
God and opened a small daycare and preschool—and Goodrich
Schools was born.

Goodrich grew steadily in its first five years, but Gideon's dreams
for the school were huge. He knew he needed additional training to
take the school to the next level. In 2014, a friend encouraged him
to consider the Sinapis program. After one year of applying what
he learned at Sinapis to his school's operations, he saw Goodrich's
enrollment nearly double to 750 students—and now he has plans to
double it again, to 1,500 students, by the end of 2017.

This growth has led to the need to acquire a second building.
He also raised $100,000 from local investors to purchase a fleet of
school buses. The school's faculty and staff increased from 40 to 105
employees as well. But the school isn't just growing numerically. In
the most recent round of standardized testing regarding educational

quality, Goodrich scored fourth out of over four hundred schools in the county.

"All over the place, God is choosing entrepreneurs. At present it is at a micro level . . . ; eventually it will go to the macro level."

Sinapis is the Latin or scientific name for the mustard seed. Courtney: "In the Bible book Matthew 13, Jesus compares the mustard seed with the kingdom of heaven. Although it is the smallest of all seeds, yet when it grows, it is the largest of garden plants and becomes a tree, so that the birds of the air come and perch in its branches. We chose the name *Sinapis*, because we want to support entrepreneurs at an early stage when they just have seeds of ideas. But we believe they can grow these seeds into strong businesses under which their communities can find rest. When they grasp early in their journey what it means to integrate their faith and their business, they will have a strong foundation, enabling them to live out their Christian values in the marketplace, show God's character, and become a blessing for many."

Courtney believes that Sinapis is one of the expressions of what God is busy doing today. She sees God's Spirit moving worldwide in the area of business: "All over the place, God is choosing entrepreneurs. At present it is at a micro level, but this is a long-term movement; eventually it will go to the macro level."

CHAPTER 9

BUSINESS AS MISSION AND THE THREE MANDATES

By Mats Tunehag

We know that businesses can fail and hurt people (Enron) and harm nature (BP). But it is equally true that we all depend on businesses, and that they can do good. The woman in Proverbs 31 was an astute businesswoman whose ventures served individuals and her community.

The Quakers practiced an expanded version of Corporate Social Responsibility (CSR) long before academics developed the term. Their motto was "spiritual and solvent": they served God and people in and through business. Even Adam Smith, the author of *The Wealth of Nations*, who is sometimes called the "father of capitalism," said that business should operate within a framework of fair play, justice, and rule of law, and that businesses exist to serve the general welfare. The computer pioneer Dave Packard said,

> Many people assume, wrongly, that a company exists simply to make money. While this is an important result of a company's existence, we have to go deeper and find the real reasons for our being. People get together and exist as a company so that they are able to accomplish something collectively that they could not accomplish separately— they make a contribution to society.[1]

In recent years, we witnessed the effects of a global economic crisis. Mahatma Gandhi's list of seven deadly social sins seems to be an accurate diagnosis for some of the causes of this crisis. There has been too much . . .

---

1. David Packard, *The HP Way: How Bill Hewlett and I Built Our Company* (New York: HarperCollins, 1995).

1. politics without principle
2. wealth without work
3. commerce without morality
4. pleasure without conscience
5. education without character
6. science without humanity
7. worship without sacrifice

We cannot, and must not, go on assuming and practicing business as usual—neither the extreme Wall Street way nor the centrally planned socially engineered way.

Did Christopher Columbus discover America? Not really. The Vikings were there many centuries earlier, even though they were not the first people on the continent. So one may say that Columbus rediscovered America. Business as Mission is not a new discovery—it is for many a rediscovery of biblical truths and practices. In one sense it is like the Reformation rallying cry of *ad fontes*, "back to the sources."

Although Business as Mission, BAM, is a new term widely used today, the underpinning concept is not. During the Reformation, old truths were highlighted and contemporary assumptions were challenged. This is what the global BAM movement is doing today. We are revisiting Scripture, questioning jargon and traditions, and assessing the situation in the world.

Many evangelicals often put an emphasis on the Great Commission, but sometimes make a great omission. This is only one of three mandates we have, which Business as Mission follows.

The first one that God gave us is the *Creation* mandate of Genesis 1–3: We are to be creative and create good things, for ourselves and others, being good stewards of all things entrusted to us, even in the physical arena. This, of course, includes being creative in business—in creating wealth. As we have seen, wealth creation is a godly talent: "Remember the LORD your God, for it is he who gives you the ability to produce wealth" (Deut. 8:18). As Christians, we often focus more on wealth distribution, but there is no wealth to distribute unless it has been created.

The second mandate is the *Great Commandment*, which includes loving our neighbor. In the first and second mandates, we find a basis for what modern-day economists call CSR, Corporate Social

Responsibility. It is about creating wealth and producing products and services in ways that are considerate of "your neighbor." CSR recognizes the importance of serving several constituencies through business—not just the owners, but also staff, suppliers, clients, community, and the physical environment. CSR includes three bottom lines and looks at the impact businesses have economically, socially, and environmentally for the various stakeholders.

We know that business can and should serve people and meet various needs. For example, unemployment is a major underlying cause of malnourishment, starvation, homelessness, disease, and limited access to medical treatment, as well as debt and crime. Providing people with jobs alleviates and prevents these dire conditions.

BAM also recognizes the importance of the triple bottom line, as it is based on the God-given mandates about being a creative steward and serving people. But BAM goes beyond this, to CSR+, as we include the third mandate, the *Great Commission*. We are to glorify God and make Christ known among all peoples. This is the fourth bottom line. As we integrate the Great Commission into our business goals, we develop a global and missional perspective. BAM is CSR+ where the + can also be seen as a cross, putting everything under the Lordship of Christ.

We need to rediscover our three biblical mandates and review their implications on church, business, and our global mission. These three mandates must be at the forefront when we plan and run BAM businesses. It is equally important that these three serve as a framework as we continuously evaluate our practical BAM mission. We must be aware of the risk of mission drift. One may start out with high hopes and ambitions regarding all three mandates, but eventually end up just operating a CSR business, fulfilling only the Creation mandate and the Great Commandment mandate. As good as that may be for various stakeholders, it is nevertheless a shortcoming. Our unique contribution and responsibility as BAMers rests on the threefold mandate. Just doing business for maximization of profit is also a mission drift. This limited understanding and praxis of business contributed to global recessions.

Mahatma Gandhi's observations on values are important as we seek the general welfare of society. As Christians in the marketplace, we strive to do business as unto the Lord, being accountable to him and to fellow followers of Jesus.

Paulo Humaitá (Brazil)

Business as Mission Accelerating in Brazil

Paulo (front left) with entrepreneurs and mentors in a leadership course.

Paulo Humaitá was on a fast career track. As manager of a company, he oversaw three hundred people at age twenty-two. A few years later, he held a key position with a global company and was asked to move to the US—a dream come true for this middle-class Brazilian. But God had other plans. Instead of moving to the States, Paulo was caught by the Business as Mission concept. He started Bluefields (http://www .bluefieldsdev.com), a business development platform, and wants to use his talents and work experiences to help start BAM businesses in Brazil and beyond. Paulo says, "I believe we have a free will and can choose, but God in his sovereignty has a plan for our lives."

When Paulo Humaitá first began working, he learned some things about "free will" while considering what he wanted to do with his life. During a search on the Internet about career planning, he read what people can accomplish when they set their minds on it. He came to realize that his career belonged to him, not the company he worked for. He became excited about the prospect of steering his life through different steps, such as aiming for clear objectives and through self-evaluation. As a result, he developed a ten-page list with career goals during all periods of his life, even until after his retirement.

We Can Plan Our Life, but God Can Open Gates

The list had become more or less an obsession, until God entered the picture. Paulo was working at a bicycle wheels and rims factory, where he led an ISO certification implementation process in the area of finance and quality. While doing so, he interacted much with leadership, employees, and unions. Meanwhile, he attended a postgraduate training in strategic planning and management, where he met strong Christian professionals. Although Paulo had grown up with church, he was currently in a lukewarm phase and not linking his faith with his work. Fellowshipping with these professionals triggered something, and Paulo started praying about his career desires. "I remember one time when I pleaded with God to open a door," shares Paulo. "He answered me: 'Son, I will not open a door. I will open a big gate.' A few weeks later, I was asked to lead the whole thing at my company and became the director of three hundred employees."

This supernatural encounter, combined with his boldness and go-getter mentality, led him to apply for a job at a multinational corporation a few years later. This was a leap of faith, since he didn't speak a word of English. Paulo: "The job interview was a disaster, since I didn't understand a thing. But I got an amazing job offer at this Danish company, Novozymes, a world leader in biological solutions. After they hired me, I immersed myself for six months in the English language, after which I traveled all over the world—to the US, China, and Europe. It was a major cross-cultural experience. Later, I heard that the vice president, who had interviewed me, told her staff afterword: 'We need to hire him!' God had opened a gate again."

Business as Mission

During one of his business travels, he attended Passion, a youth conference in Houston, Texas: "I heard about doing business in Africa; developing social growth while delivering the gospel. I heard in my heart: 'Son, that is exactly why I brought you here.' It was the strongest voice I ever heard. I got a whole new understanding that I could integrate my professional abilities and vocation with mission."

Back in Brazil, Paulo attended a mission training called Perspectives and was introduced to the concept of Business as Mission.

He researched how he could help develop a Business as Mission movement in Brazil and sought contact with national and international mission-minded networks, such as PEM (Professionals and Enterprises in Missions), AMTB (Cross-cultural Brazilian Mission), and the Lausanne Movement. "I was very excited about BAM and started speaking in churches to promote the concept."

Decision

Meanwhile, another "gate" opened: the multinational offered him a position in the US, including the possibility of a green card, a raise in salary, and other benefits. The dream to live abroad was one of the goals on his list! At the same time, the multinational also wanted him to come to Sao Paulo to become more involved with their biofuels branch. This time, however, Paulo didn't hear a clear voice from heaven and wasn't sure what to do. Then 1 Corinthians 1:27 spoke to his heart, where God says that the foolish things of the world will confound the wise. It was as if God wanted him to choose out of free will what would be considered a foolish choice in the eyes of men. "I gave my career plans to God," says Paulo. "I did get an amazing peace to stay in Brazil, and a desire and conviction to move to Sao Paulo. In hindsight, it was not a career decision but a mission decision."

Paulo gained more all-around experience at the multinational, this time learning about innovation and how to make it doable and profitable. Meanwhile, he kept speaking at churches and conferences about Business as Mission, but his frustration also grew: "I couldn't find examples of successful BAM companies ran by Brazilian entrepreneurs," shares Paulo. "My desire grew to put theory into praxis, and to start a faith-based business acceleration platform to help BAM start-ups and build an ecosystem to enable that. That's how Bluefields came into being."

In early 2016, Paulo quit his job and started Bluefields. During the first year, Bluefields kept a low profile but managed to help seven start-ups. One of them was a business idea of Joanna, a Christian Syrian refugee. After a year in Brazil, she wanted to start an Arab e-commerce business—an online shop with Arab foods, ingredients, clothes, and perfumes. Paulo: "She generates jobs for other refugees, and as a Christian she gets contacts and interacts with Arab

Muslims. I believe BAM is a great tool to gain access to minority groups, so they are able to connect with Christians and hear the gospel." Joanna's idea has grown and is fast becoming a platform to empower other refugees to develop their businesses in Brazil and overseas. Paulo: "They were recently selected between thousands of projects to join the Hult Prize in the US—one of the greatest innovative prizes in the world."

Younger Generation

As a twenty-nine-year-old, Paulo has a heart for the younger generation and wants his peers to set up BAM companies. While he knows it won't be an easy ride, he sees possibilities. "I've learned that my generation wants things fast, tends to be superficial, and is informal as they believe in equality. The gospel is for them countercultural, since it has an eternal perspective, is deep, and acknowledges the Lordship of Christ over our lives. But many of my generation are looking for meaning. Recent research shows that 65 percent of the age group between fifteen and twenty-nine isn't looking for financial safety but aims for value and self-realization through entrepreneurship."

"I've grown up with the idea that the church sends missionaries, while old ladies pray and business leaders pay," continues Paulo. "But we need to realize that all of us are missionaries. We need new models that glorify God; Business as Mission can provide such models. Bluefields wants to disciple business owners to have a kingdom-of-God-driven purpose, and we aim to help 350 business leaders by 2021. Business exists to build profit, provide employment, and create wealth; in various ways, I see therefore that business opportunities perfectly match mission needs."

CHAPTER 10

BUSINESS AS MISSION IN HISTORY

By Mats Tunehag

Although the term "BAM" may be new, the concept itself is not. It is not the latest fad or trend. We are, however, witnessing a modern-day BAM movement growing around the world, seeking to apply biblical themes and principles to the marketplace. But we are certainly not the first ones in history to do so. Thus we seek to learn from those who have gone before us. In this chapter, we will briefly look at three historical examples of BAM, although that term wasn't used. These exemplary people sought to shape their businesses with a dual perspective: for God and for people.

Transformation in Norway

Two hundred years ago, Norway was poor, most people lived and worked on farms, and the country had limited democracy and religious liberty. Today, this Scandinavian country is one of the most prosperous in the world and is renowned for its commitment to peace, democracy, and human rights. An obvious transformation has taken place, on a macro scale.

Hans Nielsen Hauge was a key agent for change. In 1796, at the age of twenty-five, he had a conversion experience. His life motto was to love God and fellow men, and he had a great gift for preaching and writing. He literally walked around the country and a spiritual revival followed.

Hauge was also entrepreneurial and started dozens of businesses. But he understood that worldview changes were needed and that the sacred-secular paradigm had to be broken down. He ensured that the businesses he started were done in community and for community. He was concerned about the unemployed and also those with handicaps. Through his pursuit of value creation, business jobs were created and communities prospered.

Hauge intentionally engaged men and women equally, both in the house churches that were formed and in the businesses that were developed. He worked on raising financial capital, and part of the profit was allocated to further grow the businesses. He was also eager to balance various bottom lines, so that various stakeholders would benefit.

Hauge also networked among numerous businesses and other groups, through which a critical mass of change agents was formed—growth that was critical for societal transformation to take place. Through his "church work," people embraced and internalized values that are essential in creating a functional marketplace. As he also engaged in legislative changes, some call him the "Father of Democracy in Norway." He was a true reformer, though it was not limited to the church arena. However, his tireless efforts in church, business, civil society, and politics brought about transformation.

Key ingredients of BAM, as well as essential elements of a BAM ecosystem, are evident in the life and work of Hauge: worldview change, breaking down of sacred-secular divide, financial capital, growing businesses, aiming at multiple bottom lines, and recognizing the multitude of stakeholders; doing business in community and for community; shaping business for God and people; creating jobs for people, including the vulnerable; intentionally working toward gender equality; recognizing the need to connect leaders and people in business, church, civil society, and politics; and networking to create critical mass in order to reach a tipping point for societal transformation.

The Quakers

The Quakers were a Christian group in the UK from the 1600s and onward. Some of them went to America to enjoy religious liberty. One of the most famous Quakers is William Penn, the founder of Philadelphia and the namesake of the state of Pennsylvania. Many

Quakers went into business and were quite successful, but they did so within a Christian ethical framework and context. Their motto was "spiritual and solvent."

They had an influence beyond their small numbers. By the early 1800s they were only 0.2 percent of the population, but four thousand Quaker families ran seventy-four banks and over two hundred companies. This includes Barclays and Lloyds.

The Quakers also did business in community for community. Anyone wanting to set up in business was "especially required to seek the consent of the meeting," and then continued to subject their business practices to the scrutiny of their peers on an ongoing basis. These things were discussed in their Christian fellowship halls.

Cadbury's Chocolate

In 1824, one of the Quaker families, the Cadburys, started a chocolate factory in Birmingham, England. This was during the industrial revolution, when many people moved into dirty and polluted cities and where exploitation of labor was common.

But the Cadbury family had an underpinning faith, which made them think and do business in an extraordinary way. They made good chocolate—still do!—and the business was profitable and grew. But they also had a concern for the well-being of their workers and their physical environment. The factory was placed outside of the city where the air was cleaner. The Cadburys built houses for the staff and provided gardens as well. The Cadbury community also included sports fields, swimming pools, and playgrounds for children, as well as heated dressing rooms and commuter transport for workers. In addition, there were morning prayers and daily Bible readings.

We can look back and see how they were intentional about creating a positive impact on the quadruple bottom line, which is talked about in the BAM movement: financial, social, environmental, and spiritual. The Cadbury story is well captured in the book *The Chocolate Wars* by Deborah Cadbury. It is one of the best BAM books you could ever read, even though it never uses the term.

The three examples above are just glimpses, and there are many untold BAM-like stories throughout history. BAM has a history that we need to explore further.

Anne Leune (Norway)

A Company Makes a Difference in a Rural Community

Anne Leune and friends. (Photo courtesy of Anne Leune)

Nordland is a rural area with some small towns in the north of Norway. Despite its awesome mountains, people relocate to urban areas. It is a challenging district because some of the locals left behind, especially the youth, are developing addictive behaviors. Anne Leune came to Nordland to participate in an outdoor-oriented Discipleship Training School with the international mission organization Youth with a Mission. The area captured her heart. She stayed and has become influential—not as a "traditional missionary" but as owner of a company, Rocks & Rivers (http://rocksandrivers.no).

Anne Leune's company offers hiking trips through the majestic nature; the activities can be anything from day-long kayaking on the river or climbing a glacier to a weeklong trip climbing through the mountains. Apart from experiencing nature, Anne and her staff offer coaching services during those trips, individually or in groups. The coaching ranges from advising companies regarding their internal communication to family counseling. Being outdoors and pushing and finding one's physical limits often provides surprising insights. Rocks & Rivers helps their customers to reflect on these. Anne shares an example: "A woman joined our adventures in nature regularly, but would always choose the easiest option when climbing a mountain or crossing a river. We started a conversation with her about this tendency, which she recognized in her daily life. She was in her thirties but still lived with her parents, even though she was irritated about her mom who seemed to treat her like a kid. The next day, we challenged her to push her limits by taking a harder route. She accepted the challenge and succeeded. This was a breakthrough for her, and this experience helped her face other challenges in her life. She initiated an honest conversation with her parents, which improved their relationship a bit. She moved out without arguments or hassle in an adult kind of way."

Over the years, many people from Nordland have been on a trip with Anne in the wild. Rocks & Rivers organizes family outings, serves local high schools and universities, and offers business outings for companies as well. In slow times, Anne has taken groups of bored youth who were hanging out on the streets for a kayak or hike. It gave her a standing with the locals, as they have come to appreciate her ability to ask, listen, and look for ways to help people take a next step. "It is an advantage that I'm straightforward," laughs Anne. "I say what I think."

Vision for Nordland

Anne has a vision for Nordland. She wants individuals to use their talents and gifts, but she also wants this for the community as a whole. She sees it as her calling to stimulate those talents. This part of Norway, with about seven thousand inhabitants, can use such impulses. Although the small towns in this area each developed their own industries, people tend to miss the boat when they don't fit into a particular type of work. This is one of the reasons why people leave to find work elsewhere. Anne: "I want to encourage innovation and creativity, so that this area will attract young people to come to work and live here, while new businesses are started."

On a small scale, this has been happening over the past years. How much influence Anne had on this development she finds hard to tell: "Influence is difficult to measure, if any and how much. Some people did share with me that I've inspired them." With her twenty-two years, she was indeed a youngster who founded an innovative business and developed a product previously unknown in the area. Only a few years later, however, influential people are asking her advice and she has been introduced to the mayor, the bishop of the

Lutheran Church, and influential businesspeople. This still surprises Anne. "Influential people call and consult me on a regular basis. They ask my opinion or how I would address an issue. It is as if they think: 'You have taken our youth out in the wild. I know I can trust you with them; now I can trust you with myself and with our local community affairs.'"

"It's more about what you do than what you say."

Influence won't just drop from the sky, emphasizes Anne. Even though she is surprised that people of standing ask her advice, she did work intentionally on a good reputation. "Influence is all about integrity. This is a small community, and people know everything about everyone. It's more about what you do than what you say. Influence is gained through perseverance and continually seizing opportunities coming your way."

The local community knows Anne and her Christian identity. Sometimes, Anne talks about her faith: "People can appreciate a conversation about God, especially when they are out in nature and become aware of their human smallness amid the majestic mountains."

Anne's faith feeds her passion for her community and gives her a goal beyond herself. After the discipleship training school with Youth with a Mission, she followed a course, Innovation and Business Administration, with a local university before she started her business. Even though a church or mission community often has similar goals and desires for the wider community, a company has a unique position as it is naturally connected with a wide range of people. Anne: "When I was active in the mission organization, my sphere of influence was limited to a fairly small circle. As a business owner, I built relationships with school leaders, youth, the government, and other companies. It is a very natural way to connect with people from different spheres of society. Being a business owner can be very strategic, when you want to see your community prosper."

CHAPTER 11

BUSINESS AS MISSION IS BIGGER THAN YOU THINK (PART 1)

By Mats Tunchag

Business as Mission, BAM, may sometimes be a tricky term due to various connotations one may associate with the words *business* and *mission*. It is, however, an important concept and an essential praxis. BAM is not a silver bullet; it is not the ultimate strategy. It is a growing global movement of Christians in the marketplace asking: How can we shape business to serve *people*, align with God's *purposes*, be good stewards of the *planet*, and make a *profit*?

Business as Mission is not trying to replace traditional means of serving God and people among all nations. Business as Mission is not a fundraising method, nor is it about attaching some church-like activities to a business. We are on a mission in and through business. It is, for example, a mission of justice. One could even say "Business as Justice." This and other terms may help us understand the holistic and transformational nature of Business as Mission.

Let me give a few brief examples, which I hope will illustrate that Business as Mission is not just doing business with a touch of "churchianity."

Business as Justice

God loves justice and hates injustice. God sent prophets again and again who spoke out against injustice, who demanded change and correction. Injustice often manifested itself in the marketplace through corruption, labor exploitation, and abuse of vulnerable people such as immigrants. To pursue honest business and care for staff is Business as Justice. To treat customers and suppliers well is also a part of this God-honoring pursuit. Business as Justice includes fighting corruption and bribery.

Business as True Religion

True worship is to take care of widows and orphans (James 1:27). These are two vulnerable groups who are still exploited in the marketplace today. Human traffickers often target lonely children, and circumstances and cunning people may force widows into prostitution.

These are realities in many parts of the world. Who will offer orphans and widows a future, giving them jobs with dignity so they can support themselves and others? The answer is Business as True Religion.

Business as *Shalom*

Shalom is a biblical concept of good and harmonious relationships, but relationships were damaged and broken through the fall in Genesis 3. Through Christ, however, there is a way to restored relationship with God, with one another, and with creation.

Business is so much about relationships with staff, colleagues, peers, customers, clients, suppliers, family, community, tax authorities, and so forth. How can we as Christians in business strive toward *shalom*, toward Business as *Shalom*?

Business as Stewardship

Every human being has been entrusted with gifts and talents. In business, we also talk about assets. Stewardship is another important biblical concept. How can we use what we have to serve? What does stewardship mean when we own and/or run a business?

God has given some people strong entrepreneurial gifts, which can be used for God and for the common good through business.

It is the same with managerial gifts or gifts of bookkeeping or sales. We should encourage people with business skills to cultivate their gifts in order to be good stewards—this is Business as Stewardship.

Business as Servant Leadership

Jesus came to serve and was an example of good and godly leadership. Many books are written on this topic, which indicates the importance of the very concept of servant leadership.

Doing business as unto the Lord means that we also explore what servant leadership means in the business context. It is not a simple formula or a cookie-cutter approach, and it may look different in different industries and cultures. But the key underlying principle is to serve people, communities, nations, and God. We are too often reminded about the lack of good leadership in the business world. Business as Servant Leadership is more than needed.

Business as Human Dignity

Every person on this planet is created in God's image. We all have value and dignity linked to the Creator. He created us to be creative, and to create good things for others and ourselves. It is deeply human and divine to create; it is an intrinsic part of human dignity. Although this creativity process—and thus human dignity—has been partly broken, there is restoration power through Jesus Christ.

It is not a sin to be unemployed, but unemployment and the inability to work and support oneself and family is a consequence of the fall. It is a loss of human dignity. Putting people to work, providing jobs with dignity is a godly act—it is Business as Human Dignity.

Marc and Sarah (Asia)

Teaching Values in Tune with God's Good Intentions

"In our company, we developed a value training program to counter prevalent negative practices," shares Marc.[1] In a predominantly Muslim country in Asia, he set up a company that produces durable goods for export. Ten years ago Marc started from scratch; since then the company has grown to around three hundred employees and has a multimillion dollars turnover.

Founding and building a company from scratch wasn't a natural choice for Marc. Trained as an engineer and with ten years of work experience in the corporate sector, he left Switzerland with his wife Sarah and two young children to work as an expatriate in an Asian megacity. That was fifteen years ago. Initially, he was involved in training technical skills to poor and marginalized youngsters. As expats, though, they were foremost expected to fundraise for projects. Marc felt from the beginning that there were more urgent needs and sustainable ways to participate in the development of this nation and its people. The country needed jobs for its huge, young

---

1. Names, country, and company have been changed or are unspecified for security reasons.

population: "They needed safe and stable work environments and a regular income," shares Marc. "Once this fundamental need is satisfied, other issues can be addressed and redressed." During a study missiology, Marc came across books on Business as Mission. "This concept expanded my horizon; I saw new possibilities and had a strong sense that this form of holistic mission in the business context was my calling."

Setting the Stage

After completing two years of service in the NGO sector, he met a North American Christian businessman who wanted to set up a factory in this particular Asian nation. The vision for creating local jobs and modeling Christ in day-to-day business work was met with a bold entrepreneurial and commercially viable manufacturing business plan. "We both had a strong sense of God's guidance," Marc says. "It was all rooted in deep mutual trust and dependency."

"[We] had a strong sense of calling, but it's good that God didn't show us what lay ahead!"

Although the stage was set, challenges lay ahead for them. "The whole business setup effort was a journey of faith that we will never forget." The endeavor was profit oriented from the beginning, but Marc did not have the business experience, or a realistic grasp of what it meant to establish a larger production company in this developing nation.

It was a steep learning curve: "I had to figure out local laws and regulations, reverse engineer products, identify processes and machines, import equipment, learn to operate the machines, and employ and train people. In addition, operating in different time zones meant communicating with the home office in North America in the evenings. I worked very long days, six days a week for several years. Sarah and I had a strong sense of calling, but it's good that God didn't show us what lay ahead! He carried us through, one challenge at a time."

Training the Staff

From the beginning, it was Marc's aim to develop, grow, and bless the company's staff. Besides growing their professional skills through the many daily hours of working together, he opted for some structured training sessions as well. The focus would be on training godly values that would benefit the company, but also help the employees in their personal lives. Marc and Sarah picked six biblical values that seemed to be neglected in the prevalent culture: "We observed, for example, that relationships between employers and employees in other factories were marked by selfishness, deep mistrust, or even hostility. So we chose to name our top value 'we work in good relationships.' Under that umbrella we taught about forgiveness, serving one another, and servant leadership. Another value was 'honesty,' in which we helped them reflect on personal faithfulness, absolute integrity with words and deeds, and—for our management staff confronted with this issue—how to deal with bribery."

Interactive

Many of their staff were illiterate, therefore Sarah used learning methods developed for illiterate learners. She used stories that the learners repeated, commented on, and sometimes enacted in role playing. The emphasis was on interactive learning through asking how that value could be applied to their daily lives at work or at home. Marc: "We were extremely focused on application rather than on knowledge. This was in contrast to local learning methods, but very key in passing on the message."

Since the prevalent culture holds the Holy Scriptures in high respect, they used biblical stories or proverbs to illustrate the company's values. A local believer with strong biblical foundations assisted them, providing cultural insights and ideas. In the training, Marc and Sarah emphasized the need for God's help when it came to the transformation of the heart. They used the Holy Scriptures with utmost respect, not hiding the source of their inspiration and teaching. At times they spoke short prayers to God using local religious forms. Marc: "It was a tightrope walk. We didn't want to exploit the employer-employee relationship in any way; we avoided religious topics in conflict with the prevalent religion or explicitly teaching salvation through Jesus alone. A couple of times some of our employees wanted to know more and we referred them to local believers. We were only blamed once—during an outburst of anger—that we were 'making Christians' in our company."

Transformation

Two key factors gradually transformed the company's culture: respectful interactions between senior management and staff, as well as the values training. "The employees became aware that our company was different," shares Marc. "I realized the change when the employees showed their trust by giving honest answers instead of telling lies to their advantage. They also started trusting me with sharing personal life stories. Change was also apparent by being greeted with warm smiles—transcending power, cultural, and gender barriers." Other indicators of change were the feedback of visiting third parties who commented how employees praised the company, or simply how employees stayed with the company long term in a context that is otherwise unsteady.

Fruits and Limits

Meanwhile, Marc and his family have returned to Europe. He is still involved in the company but in a different, less operational role. "These ten years were tough, and you can only sprint for a certain amount of time." Reflecting on the venture, Marc and Sarah feel that their company's approach of Business as Mission has brought change and blessing to many employees' lives and families. They share how it provided countless opportunities for personal witness, how it led to a group of believing employees setting up a regular fellowship and coworkers being invited to local gatherings of followers of Christ. Marc adds: "Ultimately, Business as Mission is about 'redeeming' business and having Christ reign in this sphere of society. Equally important and complementary to these efforts is church planting and church development. They go best hand-in-hand!"

CHAPTER 12

BUSINESS AS MISSION IS BIGGER THAN YOU THINK (PART 2)

By Mats Tunehag

In this chapter, we will continue to look at the correlation between business and key biblical values and concepts.

Business as Reconciliation

The apostle Paul wrote that we are agents of reconciliation. Broken relationships and conflicts are common, even in the marketplace. We also witness tension and violence between ethnic and religious groups. Can businesses provide a forum for reconciliation? Can businesspeople bridge ethnic and religious divides?

There is a long and sometimes violent history of severe distrust and tension between Muslims and Christians in Indonesia. However, I have seen firsthand how Chinese Christian businesspeople in Indonesia have changed interethnic dynamics and transformed interreligious relationships by intentionally doing business as justice, stewardship, *shalom*, servant leadership, and so forth. As God's ambassadors, we can be businesspeople on a mission to do Business as Reconciliation.

Business as Creation Care

During Creation, God conducted a daily evaluation, exercising quality control on the products he produced. His verdict was that "these are good." He has now entrusted us to be stewards of this creation. Like God, we can rejoice in being creative in the physical arena and producing goods and services that are good for people and creation. This is the first biblical mandate we have: to be creative and to work, and that includes in the business world.

The importance of environmentally friendly businesses is included in the triple bottom line, striving to have a positive impact economically, socially, and environmentally (profit, people, and planet).

On a visit to south Asia in 2012, I met a couple who works as management consultants for major manufacturing companies. This couple has a clear BAM mission, and they are able to help these companies to become more profitable, improve working conditions, save energy, and clean up huge amounts of water. Access to and preservation of clean water is one of the biggest challenges we face globally.

Creation care is not optional. Stewardship of creation and business solutions to environmental challenges should be an integral part of wealth creation through business.[1]

Business as Creation Care is essential.

Business as Loving Your Neighbor

The second biblical mandate is the great commandment to "love your neighbor as yourself." As we have seen so far in these stories, we know that business can and should serve people and meet various needs. Again, as we have seen, unemployment is a major underlying cause of malnourishment, starvation, homelessness, human trafficking, disease, and limited access to medical treatment, as well as debt and crime. Providing people with jobs alleviates and prevents these dire conditions.

Human Resource Management (a term that sounds too impersonal and technical to me) should be an expression of loving your neighbor. Taking our neighbors' physical environment into consideration as we run businesses is also a part of this responsibility. Corporate Social Responsibility (CSR) is thus not a new thing; it is based on biblical principles.

---

1. See Appendix 1: Wealth Creation Manifesto.

We can also study and learn from history. As we saw earlier, the Quakers in England and Hans Nielsen Hauge in Norway were agents of holistic transformation through business, and that was a few hundred years ago. Even then, they recognized the importance of Business as Loving Your Neighbor.

Business as Great Commission

The third biblical mandate is the global centrifugal thrust: to all peoples, to all nations. This is a major theme in the global BAM movement. How can we serve in and through business, empowered by the Holy Spirit, "in Jerusalem, and in all Judea and Samaria, and to the ends of the earth"?

> Wealth creators should be affirmed by the Church, and equipped and deployed to serve in the marketplace among all peoples and nations.[2]

Business as Mission is about being a follower of Jesus, in business and to the whole world, especially in areas with dire economic, social, and spiritual needs. This is CSR+ and this dimension is not an elective. We want to see the kingdom of God demonstrated among all peoples. It is Business as Great Commission.

Business as Body of Christ

God calls and equips some people to business. We need to affirm and encourage businesspeople to exercise their calling with professionalism, excellence, and integrity. In an "Open Letter to the Christian Nobility," Martin Luther writes:

> A cobbler, a smith, a farmer, each has the work and the office of his trade, and they are all alike consecrated priests and bishops, and every one by means of his own work or office must benefit and serve every other, that in this way many kinds of work may be done for the bodily and spiritual welfare of the community, even as all the members of the body serve one another.[3]

---

2. See Appendix 1: Wealth Creation Manifesto.
3. Martin Luther, "Open Letter to the Christian Nobility," https://web.stanford.edu/~jsabol/certainty/readings/Luther-ChristianNobility.pdf.

Business as Glorifying God

BAM is the acronym for Business as Mission, but there is another relevant acronym that describes the ultimate bottom line: *AMDG, ad maiorem Dei gloriam,* for the greater glory of God!

Melodie Cochran (Los Angeles)

It Starts with Identity—Knowing Who We Are in Christ

Melodie (left) and her prayer partner Jenni (right).

Melodie Cochran enjoys being around Los Angeles celebrities, as well as around Africa's disadvantaged. The owner of two sophisticated hair and nail salons in downtown L.A. also teaches entrepreneurship to former prostitutes in Kenya. "There is not that much difference," says Melodie. "In both worlds I encounter an orphan spirit." It is her desire that people discover the courage, creativity, and love available when they become intimate with Christ. "We teach entrepreneurship, but the foundation of the course is identity; knowing who we are in Christ."

Melodie Cochran had a remarkable journey of learning about intimacy with her Maker. Born, raised, and educated in Los Angeles, she worked for years as an electrical engineer at a middle-sized company. But in her late twenties, she felt God asking her to quit her job. "I expected it to be for a couple of weeks, before something else would come my way," recalls Melodie, but to her surprise this period lasted for seven long years.

On the Mountain

It felt like a wilderness experience; she would often sit, pray, and seek God on top of a nearby hill. The latter was not only caused by a deep spirituality, but also because she needed a break from her concerned mother. When Melodie had to move in with her due to lack of finances, she soon discovered that her mother didn't understand her choices. "You are well educated," her mother would say. "Get a job!" Melodie recalls, "I drove her crazy. Because of her job as a schoolteacher, my mom was away from home a lot; but when she would be there, I would often flee the house and go to the hills."

Melodie herself didn't understand what was going on. She kept sensing that God wanted her to be still—to listen, trust, and obey. At times she would try to find a job, but to no avail. Looking back now, though, she can value the intimate relationship developed with God during those years. "There is no stability unless you know who you are in Christ. I learned to have my identity in him, not in outward appearances like jobs, looks, and career."

Hearing God

After those years, a job as a web designer came her way and a successful career with a well-known brand followed, which enabled her to save money to start her own business. Melodie knows, however, that this long, unusual, isolated time in her life—learning to be still, to be with God, and to hear his voice—laid a foundation to her successful career as a businesswoman years later. Hearing God "talk" to her is as natural for her as any other conversation. As if it is the most common thing on earth, she shares how God told her to connect with and invest in her present business partners, who are gifted artists in their hair salon, Neihulé, but who were struggling at that time. A few years later, Melodie and her business partners bought an empty store to start a nail salon. She was convinced that God told her to do so. People warned her. Although the financial crisis had just started, and the shop was located in a downtrodden area of the city center, it turned out to be a good move. "Downtown L.A. used to be ugly and empty, but in the past years young artistic people want to live downtown. Like New York, the inner city is becoming very fast, very trendy."

The Importance of Prayer

Next to having business partners, Melodie has another partner: Jenni, her partner in prayer, ministry, and mission. Besides prayer-walking the streets of L.A. and praying for staff, clients, and suppliers, the two ladies travel together on mission trips to Europe and Africa. Connected with the Nehemiah Project, an international Christian business network, they teach vulnerable women about biblical entrepreneurship in the *banlieues* (troubled suburban communities) of Paris and slums of Kenya. Again, this idea started on the hilltop during Melodie's isolated years. At that time, she felt God wanted her to be a missionary but in a different way from what she was used to. "You won't be going as a traditional missionary, but you will go with resources. This was early 2000, and I hadn't heard about stuff like microloans. People in Africa don't need hand-outs; we need to help them develop who they are."

Mission in Africa

In 2014, Melodie and Jenni went for the first time to Kenya. They were asked by their church and a local African church to help empower former prostitutes. In a poor area where the only way for women to survive and earn a bit of money is to engage in prostitution, about a hundred and twenty were baptized in a river. Now these women questioned: "How are we going to live? We don't know what to do." The first trip wasn't that successful. The hundred people attending the weeklong training expected to get money at the end from these rich Americans.

A few months later, Melodie and Jenni returned; this time the group was smaller but serious about learning. During the week, they were taught and coached to develop business plans. Melodie: "We asked them to think of the resources they have available, and how to develop what they have. One group thought of a business plan to dry mangos. In this area, they have mango juice available but not dried mangos. They knew of a community center with a drying machine, and they included in their plan packaging the fruit, saving money, and hiring women in the future. It was a simple but entire business plan and an eye-opener for the women attending. One of them said afterwords, 'I realize now that we don't need white men to give us money.'"

Melodie and Jenni both emphasize that "it starts with identity. We focus on that in the first few days. We pray for them, receive words, pictures, and thoughts of how God sees them. This can touch them deeply. We have seen how restoring their identity in Christ gives life and brings back creativity. This village in Kenya is a tight-knit community. If some of these women realize who they are in Christ and start to develop businesses, it will have an effect on the entire village."

Vision for Los Angeles

God's mission of bringing restoration and wholeness is the mission of these two women, as much in Los Angeles as in Africa—although it looks different in their hometown, at least on the outside. The Neihulé salons are classy and have been hailed several times as among the best of L.A. This means that they are used to the scene of high-end fashion models, Grammy-Award winners, and movie stars. Melodie and Jenni pray and aim to "love people into the kingdom"—staff, clients, and suppliers. "Here in Los Angeles we suffer because of an orphan spirit, similar to what we see in the villages in Kenya."

Loving individual people, however, is just a part of their vision. They also aim to change the atmosphere of downtown L.A. by influencing it with the Spirit of the kingdom of God. They are building relationships with influential people by offering, for example, free treatments in the salons. Their prayer walks feed the vision, as they listen to the Spirit of God: What does God see? What does he want to do? What is he saying?

Prosperity with a Purpose

"We want to have influence," says Melodie. While walking downtown toward the nail salon, she points to some buildings: "We are praying about those; we envision hotels, resorts, and apartments. God wants to pour out resources—not for ourselves but with the aim to bless others. Again, it's about identity: that we know we have an inheritance as his children. God wants prosperity for us, but with a purpose. He is looking for people who are willing to wait, trust, and follow him: to change the atmosphere of our cities, so he can be glorified!"

CHAPTER 13

BUSINESS AS MISSION CAN BE SMELLY

By Mats Tunehag

Christ talks about invasion: May God's kingdom come on earth; may God's will be done in our lives and societies today. The incarnational mystery is one of engagement, living among us, sharing our lives and circumstances. Business as Mission recognizes our calling to be salt and light in the marketplace. It is not about evacuating Christians from a sinful and corrupt commercial sphere, but rather becoming an answer to the Lord's Prayer: May your kingdom come into the business world. We are a part of an invasion force, as it were.

Being involved in business, shaping it for God and the common good, will never be an easy ride or smooth sailing. But we are to pursue an incarnational witness in all our relationships and dealings in the marketplace. And, according to Thomas Merton, it may even carry an odor:

> What is holy in our midst has something to do with the odor of dung in a stable in Bethlehem, the fruity taste of wine on the table at Cana, and the smell of dried blood on the cross at Golgotha.

"... the Odor of Dung in a Stable in Bethlehem ..."

Joseph and Mary were forced to travel and make great sacrifices due to tax authorities. It was not a grand start to a relationship and family life. It was most likely stressful, disappointing, and definitely smelly. But they carried Jesus, and he transformed lives and circumstances.

Starting and operating a business can be stressful and disappointing. Dealing with tax authorities can be tough in all countries. But God's holiness can be displayed in the messiness of the marketplace. We are, like Joseph and Mary, to carry Jesus—into the marketplace.

". . . the Fruity Taste of Wine on the Table at Cana . . ."

Jesus produced wine, not just any wine, but superb quality wine. At a time of celebration, Jesus was not a party pooper. There is a time and there is a season, a time to preach, and a time to make good wine.

We want to make good quality products and excel in serving our customers. Sometimes our businesses prosper, and we can rejoice and "enjoy the good wine." God's holiness can be displayed in the smelly and dirty stable and in the festive occasions where material blessings abound.

". . . and the Smell of Dried Blood on the Cross at Golgotha."

There was a short time between Jesus' triumphant entry into Jerusalem and the mob crying, "Crucify him!" During that time, Jesus fed the hungry and healed the sick, and then he was betrayed, abandoned, put through a mistrial, and killed. There are elements of dying, of pain and hurt, even as we engage in Business as Mission. Some may sing our praises one day and intentionally try to destroy our business the next. Customers may steal and partners may cheat. Authorities may falsely accuse you of wrongdoing.

Doing business, as unto the Lord, will have "something to do with the odor of dung in a stable in Bethlehem, the fruity taste of wine on the table at Cana, and the smell of dried blood on the cross at Golgotha."

Dougald Bates (Central Asia)

Expressing the Depth and Richness of the
Gospel through Agriculture

Showing kingdom principles in all areas of business is Dougald's fo-
cus.[1] *In an area in Central Asia where corruption is a way of life, this*
New Zealander is living out another way: consistent, patient, and
determined. He believes that it will pay off in due time and that it
will be tangible, experienced in fertile lives and land: "When people
enter the goat farm I want them to see, taste, and sense God's peace
and abundance."

That is what he envisions for the future: a lush farm. In Soviet
times, this farm of six acres had been equipped with the latest tech-
nology, insulated walls, and heated barns. It was the pride of the area,
but after the collapse of the communist system anarchy reigned.
When Dougald found it in 2014, everything had been taken and the
windows were broken. "But the roof was still there!" he says with
a smile. He bought the place in partnership with a local, who had
become a Christian. Now in their first year in business, they have
twenty goats with plans to increase to over a hundred in the years to
come. The farm could eventually handle up to a thousand.

Dougald is visiting Western Europe to buy semen from the
French who raise goats in the Alp Mountains. "Their goats are less
productive, but used to changing climates. We need that. We live in

---

1. Names and places have been altered for security reasons.

a rough place and I figure better a less productive goat than a dead one," he says with a sense of understatement. The climate and nature are rough, as are other circumstances—such as red tape, bureaucracy, and corruption. On top of that, his New Zealand connections don't have expertise in the part of Central Asia where Dougald and his family reside. As a result, he can't easily order needed equipment and have it shipped over: "The infrastructure between these parts of the world is nonexistent."

"God Wired Us This Way"

Dougald and his wife raised their family in a Central Asian country whose people are mostly followers of Islam. The country is one of the poorest and hardest in the area, yet Dougald believes that God especially designed them for this kind of place: "We know how to filter water, make food from scratch, and have learned to be in temperatures of minus 23 while the power fails. We have always loved being in rural and rough places. God wired us this way; it suits us and we think it's fun." He laughs. "My wife likes it even more than I do."

Genuine Involvement

Missions and development are also part of their genes. Dougald's parents were missionaries and his in-laws were involved in aid and development. After their marriage and his studies in agriculture, Dougald and his wife discovered that the mission agency Interserve suited them best: "They integrate work and missions. Other agencies argued that teaching English or computer skills would give me a platform to get into a country. But I don't want 'an excuse' to get in; that's deceptive to me. My aim is to be genuinely involved. I love agriculture and believe that God desires to use all of our natural gifts and talents."

Developing Trust

After language studies in the capital city, they set up an NGO, became active with irrigation, and moved to a rural area because they wanted to focus on a displaced minority group. Dougald and his family worked with the aim to improve the local irrigation system. They promoted a system of transparency, efficiency, and equity, where people would measure the amount of water they used and pay accordingly, rather than the poor bearing far more than their fair share. It would enable the vulnerable, particularly single mothers, to access water.

However, this undermined corrupt and anarchistic forces: it meant less income for the ones in charge, because it revealed that the water used by the rich was being charged to the poor. It also meant that the farmers needed to respect the system and not break it whenever they wanted water.

Seeing only a glimmer of progress was disheartening, considering the huge effort they and their local staff put in. Yet they highly valued the progress they saw in their relationships: "We developed trust with the people, as they saw that we were genuinely involved with them and seeking their welfare. They did acknowledge that the system we developed would bring more fairness and prosperity, but they weren't prepared to change local practices. It made us realize that peoples' hearts need to change first, before improvement can last."

Next to their agricultural work, Dougald and his wife helped with Bible translation into the local language. They would regularly have local people living with them, and they noticed often that befriended Muslims initially became more serious about their own faith. Dougald: "I see that as positive thing, as a sign that God is beginning to work in them. When God is touching their hearts, they want to know and experience God in the way a Christian does and they feel convicted that their actions and words should line up. At first, they often try to do this in the only way they know how: by trying to become a better Muslim, by praying and fasting more. We pray that they will realize that they cannot make their hearts clean, and share with them the amazing sacrifice God gave to set them free. It can take a long time for people to be willing to count the cost and accept Jesus. We had two girls living with us in the first years when we were living in the city; these girls have had dreams of Jesus appearing to them, and they know the gospel to be true, but it is difficult for them to be open about it. In their circles, becoming a Christian is considered blasphemy: 'Muslims should know better,' they argue; since the prophet Mohammed came after Jesus, a Muslim is considered to 'go backwards' when they decide to follow Jesus."

From NGO to Business

One of the employees working with him in the NGO became a Christian, and Dougald saw his character changing. While looking for a way to disciple this man and to enable him to stay within his community, an opportunity arose to buy land and start a farm. Dougald had realized for a while that the country desperately needed local production. "Everyone is buying and selling; they start a shop or a restaurant, but the country needs a broader base of income. They need production and manufacturing businesses that can provide income and jobs. The men go to Russia, because of lack of available work. They often have a second wife in Russia or just disappear. It is breaking families apart and causing all kinds of social problems."

Seeking out the possibilities, the family decided to turn their dairy goat hobby into a farm. Locals have a strong belief that goat milk has medicinal and healing properties, yet it is almost impossible to source as there is no dairy goat industry. Together with their local partner, they purchased the run-down former Soviet dairy farm and registered a business. They see the business not only as a way to provide useful and fulfilling work to people, but also as the context where discipleship can be lived out.

A Productive Meeting

Dougald shares his coworkers' witness God at work—that it is possible to follow and trust God, and to go against local practices. In closing down the NGO and starting the business, a taxman looked through their books and wanted twelve thousand dollars. Dougald knew someone above him, higher in the hierarchy, and could have gone to that person to force the taxman to drop the charges. Instead, he decided to go a different way—a way of trust, faith, and love: "I realized that by going to his superior I would enforce the local system by shaming him. Instead, I decided to trust God. I took the time for this meeting and shared with the taxman that I loved him and his country, while explaining that I was there to start a business to serve the country. I also shared about my walk with God and that all our money belongs to this God, whom I serve. I continued to explain that if he took that money he would be stealing from God, but God would take care of me and the business, as I have witnessed that God had done that before. I also shared the story in the Bible, where a coin was found in the mouth of a fish when tax money was needed." It was a time-consuming meeting, and the whole process took three days of Dougald's time. The taxman eventually came back to them with the notification that he had dropped the charges to a few hundred dollars and apologized, with the explanation that if he didn't charge something his superiors would take the books to go through them, as they expected him to find something. "Such time-consuming interactions to battle corruption do frustrate me from time to time," Dougald admits. "That week, though, that meeting was the most productive thing I could do!"

Corruption

"Corruption is everywhere and on every level," continues Dougald. "In the NGO world, local people seeking a job have to bribe to have their CV admitted. The office manager won't let your CV come through when you don't pay him. Even though I continually checked, I couldn't be sure there was no bribery in my NGO."

Dougald tells about a board member of the water association with which he was working who abused his position: "While people knew what he was doing and would admit that it was not right, they wouldn't speak up, because they knew they would do the same in his situation. It is just easier to go along with the system; everybody has their own position in the system, but they are all victims of it, especially vulnerable people like widows who don't have the money to pay the ones in charge. You may have water today, but you are not sure if it is allowed tomorrow. Everyone and every department works for himself." Dougald adds, "Satan is in the system; he is the destroyer of order and doesn't want people to work together and cooperate for the common good."

Committed to Integrity and Discipleship

Dougald is convinced that integrity and honesty will pay off in the kingdom that God has already begun establishing. Those are the seeds he aims to plant in the ground. He recognizes, however, the inherently difficult business environment and that this approach does not guarantee earthly business success. He has lost a business before, when they were new in the country. They grew mushroom spawn in their basement, with plans to distribute the seed to vulnerable people, for them to grow it. Dougald grew the spawn in a well-to-do part in the city in the cellar of an apartment complex. This area had no power failures, which was important to grow the seed that needed a constant temperature and ventilation. But a well-to-do neighbor didn't like them and made sure they had to leave, even though they had all the needed paperwork. They considered picking up the mushroom business again, but they realized it was vulnerable for bribery, due to being such a perishable product. "When a truck is stopped for too long, the mushrooms wither and die. People will find out quickly, and that makes you vulnerable."

Dougald is deeply committed to integrity, even when it means losing a business, or when it takes ten times longer. "The local people are searching. They see the bad economic situation. They see their leaders go on pilgrimage to Mecca, but meanwhile repeating corruption, staying in dishonesty, and stripping off their people." Dougald realizes that it takes a great deal of time to change systems. With every meeting and personal encounter, it's as if a mustard seed of integrity is planted in the ground. "I won't give any bribes to encourage them to do something they shouldn't; to jump steps, to favor, or to disregard standards. Instead, I encourage them to do their work because it is good for the country, because they love their job and love their country. Once in a while I might give a very small gift like a box of chocolates to show appreciation, but only after they have done a good job."

Discipleship

Even though the seed is planted, Dougald isn't sure if it will grow: "You can instill Christian principles, like I did while working with the water system, but when the hearts of the people don't change, the principles will go with you when you leave. It won't stick."

In his partner—who has decided to follow Christ—he found fertile ground. Dougald's aim is to disciple people like him by walking together following God: "Situations like the encounter with the taxman was an intense level of character development for me and my partner, because we weren't sure of the outcome. In those kind of real situations, discipleship moves from knowledge to obedience and experiencing God's faithfulness. My partner then shares those experiences with his unsaved relatives and other workers who live at the farm."

"We serve a God who . . . is genuine."

Their earlier resolve to be genuinely involved in the country, instead of "having an excuse to be there," moved to another level as they learned how Christians were viewed as workers. "In the earlier years in the city, I really wanted to hire local Christians but was reluctant to do so. Christians often thought they were hired only to evangelize rather than to complete the work they were paid for. Their Muslim counterparts worked much harder, but what a shameful witness! By doing so, we *tell* people about Jesus, but by our lives we tell that what we *do* isn't important. But that's as much a witness. We serve a God who isn't phony. On the contrary, God is genuine. He reveals himself as I Am. God is who he says he is."

Expressing the Fullness of God's Kingdom

"We need to demonstrate God's genuineness, who he is in himself," continues Dougald. "I want my workers to wear safety goggles when welding, because I care and God cares about their eyes and their health. Those kinds of things are a part of my faith. Christian faith has to be real, demonstrating God's kingdom in all areas of life and business."

Developing the goat farm is a true faith journey: with love and integrity showing another way of life in a multitude of areas, next to getting equipment and finances to build the place. For Dougald and his wife, it is all worth it. They bought six hectares (about fifteen acres), and recently local authorities allocated another eight hectares (about twenty acres) of land to them. In one way this was a miracle, and in another way it shows that locals recognize and appreciate their good intentions. Although Dougald realizes there is still a long road ahead of them, he is holding onto his vision with determination: "I want to show what is possible; I want the farm to be a tangible witness of what can be possible when we are in relationship with a living and loving God."

CHAPTER 14

BUSINESS AS MISSION IS A CENTRIFUGAL FORCE

By Mats Tunehag

We need to act on Christ's command and address real needs, as well as deploy businesspeople to serve among all peoples of the earth. To do this, we need to be less centripetal and more centrifugal. Centripetal is a force moving inward, toward the center. Centrifugal is a force moving out from the center. Let me use an analogy.

When we cook, we take the saltshaker and pour salt over the meat. As absurd as it may seem, there is another way of cooking. One could try to squeeze the meat through the small holes into the saltshaker and thus make the meat salty. We as Christians are called to be salt. Let the saltshaker represent the church and the meat represent the world into which Christ sends us.

Unfortunately, we are too often preoccupied with trying to get people to the church building and to be involved in some program—often held in the very same building. Many churches have a centripetal focus. It is as if we are trying to squeeze the meat into the saltshaker. We ought to be more centrifugal and consider how we can be salt in the marketplace, and how we can pray for Christians who own and operate businesses.

The church should be thankful for having "salty members" out there in the business world. People with a calling to business are a hybrid, as it were, of a businessperson and a missionary: that is, a "bizzionary."

Paul Unsworth (London)

Reinventing Church Downtown in Multicultural London

"I've had more significant conversations in this coffee shop in one week than a whole year working in a church building," says Paul Unsworth. "We need new models of church, where people can have a sense of belonging regardless of what they believe." In a busy, multicultural and popular street in East London, this Baptist pastor is reinventing church. He and his team started a commercial coffee shop—as a church—and they learned some lessons on the way.

In June 2012, the coffee shop opened its doors in Brick Lane, East London. In this area, twenty thousand people visit the shops and market on a regular Sunday. Many kinds of faiths are shared, but Christians are hardly to be found. While walking here one Sunday, Paul Unsworth realized that they needed "to be here, among these crowds." They named the coffee shop Kahaila (http://kahaila .com), which is wordplay with the Hebrew *Kahila*, which means "community," and *Chaim/hai*, which is connected with "life." These words represent their purpose of bringing life to the very center of the community: to plant a church as a café.

Paul says, "Traditional churches work well for Christians, but we want to explore how we model a church that engages people outside the church—those kinds of people who view a church as a red telephone box: an amazing part of our heritage. They don't want these telephone boxes removed and love to see them standing somewhere in a street, but they will never use them. They look at church the same way: they love the architecture and the fact that it is part of British culture, but it's not for them."

No Business, No Mission

The whole coffee shop endeavor did cost a lot of money and effort. Over a hundred thousand pounds were invested, partly donated and partly borrowed. This meant they had to run the business well in order to raise an income and to attract clients. Their aim was to become one of the best coffee shops in London, and they seem to be well on their way: nearly four times as much profit was made as initially anticipated. But what's more, people are finding them and recommending Kahaila on the Internet for their good coffee, food, service, and atmosphere—while regularly adding the comment, "Oh, and these guys are Christians."

"We don't have Christian music playing or crosses on the wall," Paul explains, "since we want non-Christians to encounter people, not religious artifacts. Neither do we want to be a Christian hangout. Instead, we want to connect with people who aren't coming to church; with them we want to build a relationship. We give attention to our coffee and food; that needs to be good, and we need to give good services. When we don't have a thriving business, we don't have clients, and therefore we don't have a mission."

If the business fails, then the mission fails.

Wednesday Night Church

The heart of Kahaila is the community of faith running the place. On Monday mornings, they start the week with prayer. On Wednesday nights, they have the church service at the coffee place. In the beginning, Paul closed the shop in the late afternoon, and then reopened it a bit later, but that didn't feel right. Now they invite the customers to attend. "Stay for our church service, I tell people. People are surprised; the invitation catches them off guard and opens up for a conversation."

Relationships and Bonding

The community members continuously experiment with different events: "We had board game evenings, but they didn't last. When it doesn't work, we try something else. The evenings with live music go well, as well as the 'bring-and-share supper club' and the book club. For the book club, we don't choose particular Christian books but books that stimulate conversations about life."

The aim of Kahaila is to create a neutral space for the so-called generation Y, born in 1982 and later. This generation is not hostile toward church; they just think it's not for them. "Their friends are not religious; the church is outside their social circle. This generation wants to belong, before they believe, but the church is often centered on belief. So how, and where, can this generation of non-Christians start to feel they belong?"

"How, and where, can this generation of non-Christians start to feel they belong?"

This sense of belonging is indeed happening. "Why didn't you invite me?" a customer asked when he heard that the faith community went away for a weekend. Paul says, "He visited the shop regularly, but had told us that he was an atheist, so we hadn't invited him for our weekend with a focus on prayer and worship. But his comment made sense. He had become our friend. He felt he belonged, and therefore it was natural for him to come along, so we told him he was welcome to join." The atheist admitted after the weekend that the prayer and worship "had got to him."

"Church Is a Way of Life"

Paul believes that the church is not an event or a statement of faith: "Church is a way of life. Jesus said 'follow me.' Following Jesus is about real-life situations. So we don't tell someone like this friend, who has become interested in the faith, to join now a regular church as we know it on Sunday. We would be sending him into an alien culture."

"Christians need to be deprogrammed," Paul continues. "They often feel guilty when they don't witness. We need to learn to be normal; not to force a conversation about faith, but to ask questions that show our genuine interest in them as a person. They in turn will want to know things about us; in a natural way, this can create opportunity to talk about faith. It's about relationship and friendship, which happens here on every level. Clients will ask the folks behind the counter how their day has been. After some time, the café has become busier, which has made it harder to have these kinds of conversations. So now, we purposely overstaff. From a business point of view, we could not afford to do this; therefore, we work with volunteers from a mission agency to be able to give clients the same attention."

> "Christians need to be deprogrammed; they often feel guilty when they don't witness."

Before starting Kahaila, Paul was a youth pastor within evangelical circles. But he grew up in a non-Christian background, and his desire for the Christian faith to be known by and be relevant for his generation motivates him to seek ways beyond how it's done within church walls: "Traditional church as we know it might be good for Christians; but to be more accessible to non-Christians, we have to be prepared to sacrifice some of what we love about the more traditional model of church. I, for example, have to give up preaching, which I love. Instead, we usually have discussions, as it enables people to engage with Scripture for themselves, and it also enables non-Christians to dialogue and ask questions. There are some really big churches in this area, but the people attending come from somewhere outside the area and are not engaging with anyone in this neighborhood. New expressions of church need to be incarnational and connect with people in the community."

Much More Is Going On

The neighborhood is aware that there are Christians to be found in Kahaila. A Muslim, who worked in a shop nearby, came to ask if they could pray for him because he needed a visa. They did so, there and then. Apparently he got his visa, because he was no longer seen in the neighborhood. "We like to see end results," Paul says, "but often we don't see it. We need to learn to think long term also about our influence in the neighborhood."

"Loving is a way to make disciples."

Paul admits he was a bit disappointed the first months after the opening of the shop, since no one had yet come to faith. But as he prayed, he felt the Great Commission of making disciples could be accomplished by obeying the Great Commandment "to love God and love your neighbor as yourself." Paul says, "We are loving our neighbors and relationally engaging with them; loving is a way to make disciples. John 13:35 says, 'By this everyone will know that you are my disciples, if you love one another.' So how do we actively love the people who come into the café and who are in the local community?"

New Leaders Empowered

Meanwhile, young leaders involved with Kahaila are empowered and starting new ministries. Paul likes to encourage and help them into whatever God has placed on their hearts. Some started a mentoring and education program in a local prison. Others started a network among women who are trafficked into prostitution, which developed into setting up a safe house called Ella's Home.

Entrepreneurship is part of Paul's DNA, and being in contact with the vulnerable women victimized by trafficking ignited the idea to start Luminary Bakery, where these women can have a decent job, and where they can learn within a safe community and connect with Christians. Paul says, "We need business for these women, because they need jobs. We sell much cake in the café, so we decided that starting our own bakery could be another profitable business."

Being involved in the needs of the city and seeking ways to help solve problems opens up connections with different people in the city. Paul is convinced that they "need to get involved. We need to think about the big issues in our city and our world. What are they? We shouldn't rely on government or church money but create new ministry models. We can connect with others and work together, while unashamedly following Jesus. It all starts there—with a love for God and people, and a desire that justice is restored."

CHAPTER 15

CHRONOS AND *KAIROS*

By Mats Tunehag

Business as Mission is not a technique. It is a worldview and a lifestyle. It is about following Jesus in the marketplace and to the ends of the earth, loving God and serving people through business. BAM is not doing business with a touch of "churchianity." BAM is not Christians just doing social enterprise. BAM recognizes God as a stakeholder who has a vested interest in the *multiple bottom lines* and *multiple stakeholders.*

BAM must be underpinned by a biblical worldview, which informs our planning, operations, and evaluations. One critical aspect of worldview is time, as this has implications on what we can do and on what God does. Time affects how we plan, operate, and evaluate a BAM business, aiming at a positive impact on multiple bottom lines for multiple stakeholders. As we do this, there are extremes to be avoided: that is, quantifying and monetizing everything or nothing.

We need to ask: How can God be a stakeholder in our business? How can we aim at a kingdom-of-God impact in and through business? This is where *chronos* and *kairos*, which are two Greek words for "time," come in.

- *Chronos* is quantitative, sequential, and of course related to the word *chronological.* We operate in the *chronos*; it is where we plan and evaluate our businesses. It's where we live our day-to-day lives.
- *Kairos* is qualitative, the supreme moment, the right time. This is used for God's intervention, in the fullness of time. We cannot control this, but we can set the stage for it to some extent.

We can learn from Daniel and his three friends in Babylon who were involved in civil service as mission. In the first six chapters of the book of Daniel, we observe:

- Daniel and his friends served God and the nation with professionalism, excellence, and integrity. They served in the *chronos*.

- God used this stage set in the *chronos* to occasionally intervene (*kairos* moments), bringing glory to himself and transforming people and nations.

- Most days for Daniel and company, however, were just another day, week, year, or decade in the office. It was their faithful and good work (in the *chronos*) that set the stage for miracles and changed lives; in the right moment and in his own time, God intervened (*kairos*).

This is essential as we run BAM businesses. How can we serve our customers, staff, and suppliers with professionalism, excellence, and integrity? We can and should carefully plan, execute, and evaluate accordingly.

We also need to understand that we cannot convert anyone by pushing through or forcing a spiritual impact. So what steps can we take in the *chronos* to set the stage for *kairos*? Or in the words of the apostle Paul, "I planted, Apollos watered, but God caused it to grow."

Like Daniel and his friends, we must be prepared for another day, week, year, and decade in the business. No matter how mundane the day-to-day can seem, we must remind ourselves that we are constantly and intentionally shaping our business for God and people, for various stakeholders and multiple bottom lines.

Chronos and *kairos* can help us to plan and set reasonable expectations, as well as help us to see the role we can play in what God does. Having this view of time should encourage us to relax and trust God. We plant and water, but God will bring life and growth.

Patrick McDonald (Oxford)
Being Globally Involved—Scaling God's Mission

"God is serious about business," says Patrick McDonald. "Jesus is un-wavering in his pursuit of life, justice, wholeness, and beauty in this world." Profoundly convinced of this truth, Patrick seeks to forward God's mission by supporting entrepreneurs starting and scaling up their initiatives. After many years of involvement in charity, he recognized some of its built-in limitations and embraced business as a tool to achieve greater impact.

Patrick McDonald has an impressive portfolio. As a teenager, this Danish-born activist was already working and caring for street kids in Bolivia. He went there shortly after a touching encounter with Christ during the week his father died. While in Bolivia and experiencing the overwhelming needs of street children, Patrick saw that more could be done when local children's ministries improved their standards and worked together. That's why he started Viva. This charity equips, resources, and connects urban slum churches that help children at risk. Based in the UK, Viva works on a local and global level, and is supported by a great number of international Christian relief organizations. Because of this involvement, Patrick began to know the charity world from the inside out.

"I Lost My Youth, My Inheritance, and My Dignity"

Over the years, he has started to realize the built-in limitations of present-day global charity. He compares it with building the Eiffel Tower with a screwdriver: "The tools don't fit the job. I lost my youth, my inheritance, and my dignity, trying to raise money to help desperate children around the world. It took 80 percent of my time; it was a never-ending and deeply unpleasant challenge. I'm well educated, have the best technical tools available, work hard, and can be persuasive. Despite our best efforts, we could never raise enough. If it is that hard for me, it must also be hard for others."

Stolen Batteries

Because of this mismatch between goal and tool, Patrick found that charity is too often an environment where creativity doesn't have room to develop. "In the world of charity, I know a lot of amazingly talented people, real 'wow' guys and girls. But I often felt as if someone had stolen their batteries. That is understandable, because when children are dying and there is hardly anything you can do, that results over time in some kind of burnout. You stay there because of commitment, but you don't go to work to win simply because you know you very often can't. When you see little fruit from your work, you miss out on the dynamics of delivering something significant."

"Please understand me right, I love charity," Patrick emphasizes. "I try and give more and more money away each year as a proportion of my income. Charity is about local and human involvement, just as Jesus told us in the story of the compassionate Samaritan. It is about responding generously to the many needs around us with money, time, and creativity." Yet experiencing the limitations of present-day practices brought him into a crisis, and Patrick was tempted to dial back his expectations to almost zero: "Believe me, the option to retreat to the back seat of the church and forget about the Great Commission was very tempting. My flesh said yes! It's just too hard and not a fair fight. It's too humiliating as sons and daughters of the Living God to simply not reflect the power of Jesus in our work."

Questioning How Things Are Done

The conviction of the greatness of the Living God fed his search, mixed with having experienced the enormous needs in the world. It stretched his mind and made him question prevalent ways of thinking and doing. If the Maker of everything gave his sons and daughters the task to be salt and light, to bring justice and transform societies, then he would surely provide the ability and means to do so—much more effectively. Patrick: "I want to do more, be more, and see more things happen that put a smile on the face of Jesus. God is big and able—and wants us to build projects that reflect that."

Openwell

In 2012, his search led him to start Openwell (www.openwell.co) in Oxford. "During my many years at Viva, I had learned a lot about getting good things started," continues Patrick. "I had also seen many wonderful projects needing help to effectively launch." At that time, Patrick also felt that he could best serve Viva by stepping down as CEO, and he felt drawn into using his knowledge and contacts to help other missional entrepreneurs get started and /or grow the impact of their work. "We provide entrepreneurs with two things: advice and access to capital. 'We' are a growing team of former chief executives supported by a powerful consulting team and the emergence of a corporate capital function."

Patrick continues, "We recognize that good ideas can come from many places: Christian missionaries, MBA students, innovation units in large corporates. For us, the source of the idea doesn't matter as much as its quality and the quality of the entrepreneurs." Openwell aims to combine expertise from multiple sectors, bringing the "heart" and "hands" of charity together with the "head" and "feet," as well as the strength and speed of the worlds of business and finance.

For example, the Openwell team is involved with an international corporation to help develop a project in the slums of Nairobi, Kenya. By enabling locals to sell a product of this corporation, their aim is to help them to handle money and eventually start their own shop. So far, it has created livelihood for five hundred people in a sustainable and profitable way. Meanwhile, other internationals are asking their advice on how to expand their market while benefitting people and the planet. Patrick says, "It is about helping big business use what they are good at to help people and the planet, by growing into new markets and creating new offerings—not just about giving something away or sending people out to paint picket fences."

Redeeming Business

It brought him to embrace business and see its potential, but before Patrick could do so, his own way of thinking about business needed to be renewed. His assumption was that business was inherently bad: "I thought it was all about self-seeking and self-enrichment; about big corporations polluting and destroying the planet while creating value for the shareholder. 'Creating value for the shareholder' is indeed part of the truth, but every good lie has a part of the truth. It is true that a human being has an arm, but so much more besides that. Equally, it is true that business relies on profits, but equally so much more."

> *"Part of the body of Christ is called to business, but they don't hear the call, because they don't want to be part of what they perceive to be a destructive arena. . . . We need to redeem business."*

Patrick thinks the idea that business is inherently bad is widespread within the church: "In a church gathering of five hundred, only three people stood when asked the question if they were in business. Part of the body of Christ is called to business, but they don't hear the call, because they don't want to be part of what they perceive to be a destructive arena. They feel that by being in business, they abandon their first calling to love Jesus." They think: 'I share my faith privately, and when I'm the owner I can apply Christian principles and do things slightly differently.' I think there is for business much more fundamental things to do; we need to redeem business!"

Business Exists for Prosperity

Patrick is convinced that business is meant to create wealth and prosperity in a broad sense: socially and materially. "Prosperity is a lot more than money. It is also about social and human capital. When I treat my partner badly, I lose relationships. My staff is human capital. At Openwell we're on a journey, and I want my colleagues to prosper—not manipulate them, but instead grow human capital."

Business should help to create a beautiful world, which lifts our spirits. Patrick relates this to the outward force of the gospel: "We are being sent to heal the sick, build good systems, and make a beautiful city. A congregation might be called to reach and rebuild an entire neighborhood, but in doing so they would need to work constructively together with the local authority, the business community, and other stakeholders. There is no reason why a number of kingdom businesses can't be an integral part of such a transformation program and work across a number of cities to achieve God's vision for the area. Our message lacks credibility if we reduce the work of the church to preaching and teaching, and our impact becomes less than what Jesus is after. That said, I agree that the most important thing for the church is evangelism and discipleship—equipping the saints—everything else flows from there."

"Grow Up!"

On the website of Openwell, there is no reference to the Christian faith. When Patrick is asked if they did this deliberately, since the Christian faith might cause offense in a Western secularized context, he explains: "You want the most redemptive and valuable source in life—the Lord Jesus Christ—to be present. Why kick him out? That's bad for business. We're transparent about it. 'Causing offence'? That's cowardice! We shouldn't be ashamed of the gospel. Grow up. It's childish to somehow put Jesus in a box or hide him in a cupboard. Jesus is a real and present reality. If doors are shut because people are offended, I count that as a blessing. That said, if we put lots of 'Jesus-speak' all over our website, then we raise unnecessary questions from our secular partners and peers. Anyone who works with us will soon know why we do what we do, but we might never work with them if we appear as a Christian mission on our website. I recognize this is a balance, but one that we so far seem to have achieved. Pray for us that we get this right!"

Intense and Light

Although Patrick has an intense personality, there is a remarkable lightness about him. He is filled with passion, but instead of a "passion to push," he seems to see and hear something to follow and pursue. Patrick: "God is the originator of great ideas; he cares about making good and beautiful things and places. Jesus is the primary pursuer of justice; he cares about prisoners who come out of prison to no fixed abode. If it bothers Jesus, it should bother us! It's about achieving the aims of the king. There are lots of amazing people with great ideas out there; they have *God ideas*. They are touched by a call to do something. We help them resource it, so that world-changing ideas can reach their full potential."

CHAPTER 16

BUSINESS WITHOUT MISSION

Not Good for Long-Term Impact

By Mats Tunehag

Should Christians in business have a Jesus-centered mission as they do business? Or should they just practice good business ethics but play down Jesus in their business relationships and activities?

Some like the term "Business as Mission," and others dislike it. Whatever the terminology used, it is the concept that is important. We believe that business should aim at more than just the three bottom lines, often cited in Corporate Social Responsibility (CSR) as economic, social, and environmental. Business as Mission includes these but goes beyond, drawing from a kingdom-of-God theology. This wider perspective includes Jesus and the Great Commission. The kingdom of God is our mission.

Some use the term "Business for Transformation," which also reflects our belief and mission: businesses can and should be instruments for holistic transformation of people and societies. Business on a transformational mission! Transformation—good and lasting change—takes time.

Can we learn something from missionaries and Christian cross-cultural workers of the past? Is there a difference in long-term impact between different kinds of missionaries? The results of a fourteen-year-long research project have surprised many, but the evidence is clear and overwhelming: there is a correlation between Jesus-centered conversionary missionaries and democratic development, better health, lower corruption, greater literacy, higher educational attainment, and a stronger civil society.[1]

Sociologist Robert Woodberry and about fifty research assistants spent many years gathering and analyzing material from several continents. They assumed that missionaries might have contributed toward a positive long-term impact in communities, but they were wrong. The missionaries were not just part of the process, they were central to it; they were the most crucial factors for the positive developments. To date, over a dozen other studies and reports have confirmed Woodberry's facts and conclusions.

But there is more to this story. They weren't just any kind of missionary or Christian aid worker. The previously mentioned positive effects of missionary work applied only to *conversionary missionaries*. These Jesus-focused missionaries were not linked to colonial authorities. They unashamedly believed that people should hear about Jesus. They tried to meet physical and social needs, and they engaged in justice issues and fought oppression. Missionaries who had been hired by the state apparatus or linked to power structures did not have this long-term impact.

That said, not all missionaries or mission initiatives have been exemplary. But the good and long-term influence on the macro level cannot be denied. The evidence of causal correlation between conversionary missionaries and holistic transformational impact is persuasive.

Woodberry's study also shows that these missionaries in general did not set out to reform societies, but—driven by love for Jesus and people—their work had a far greater impact than they had dreamed. There is, of course, a need for more research, and this report does not mean we should uncritically celebrate all missionary activity.

But these findings should cause us to review and further discuss our mission, whether we call it Business as Mission, Business for Transformation, or nothing in particular.

There is not a one-size-fits-all approach, or just one way of being a follower of Jesus in the marketplace. We need to be tactful and

1. Andrea Palpant Dilley, "The Surprising Discovery about Those Colonialist, Proselytizing Missionaries," *Christianity Today* (January 8, 2014), http://www.christianitytoday.com/ct/2014/january-february/world-missionaries-made.html?paging=off&utm_source=hootsuite&utm_campaign=hootsuite.

also mindful of culture and security-related issues. Though, at the same time, we should learn from those who have gone before us: Jesus-centered missionaries were instrumental in bringing about holistic transformation.

We mustn't be or do business without a mission.

Kees de Zwart (The Netherlands) and John (Asia)
Being Available and Staying Close to Jesus

In a closed country located on the Asian continent, Christians are the outcasts of society. They have great difficulty finding jobs and are excluded from good education. In this country, Dutchman Kees de Zwart established a business providing vocational and discipleship training. He is doing this with a local partner, John.[2] "Our aim is to empower the church to nurture new believers," says Kees. "Many of them came to Christ after they had a revelatory dream." Kees believes that the idea for this business itself was inspired by supernatural intervention.

During a walk along the Dutch coast in the sandy dunes, Kees de Zwart heard the words *missionary partnership* and the names of three countries. "I heard a voice, looked around me, but I saw no one," Kees recounts. "It was bizarre. I wondered if illusion had taken the best of me. I had never been in the three countries mentioned, so I decided to refrain from action and just wait and see. If this was really of God, he would confirm it."

It was confirmed: within three weeks, Kees had a connection in each of the three countries.

---

2. Kees's partner's name has been changed and the country is unspecified for security reasons.

Christians in a Closed Country

After two years, in close cooperation with his local partner John, he started a business in one of the countries, which was a rather dangerous place. Kees says, "When you evangelize there, there is a good chance of death or severe hostility. As a result, lots of Christians have a victim mentality; they are under threat and have little or no protection. Others, like my local partner, are growing stronger. He faces hostility and opposition but has developed a tremendous trust in God. Through our business, we want to help Christians get rid of their victim mentality; we want to make them strong enough to mature their faith, because the number of Christians is growing rapidly. Jesus reveals himself to people in their dreams, and they receive guidance like: 'Go to that shopkeeper or that neighbor; he will tell you more about me.'"

Empowering Christians

The goal is to empower Christians through discipleship as well as through professionalization. Discipleship training is combined with top-level training, preparing participants to work as skilled professionals for high-end firms in the region. In addition, they receive training in business to enable them to have their own businesses. Kees says, "We started in 2015 with fourteen students; by the end of that year, their number had increased to forty. They are very enthusiastic and eager to learn, both professionally as well as spiritually."

Background

Kees is owner of the Vanderperk Groep in the Netherlands, a business in publishing, printing, communication, and web design. Over the years, he has increasingly used his business as a base for missions: he hires local disadvantaged persons, helped start a publishing house for Christian publications in Cuba, and initiated trips to developing countries to expose business colleagues to global needs. However, his recent venture together with his local partner (who became a close friend) has another dimension. "The question was if I would be prepared to engage fully in Business as Mission, including all the risks it would take. A significant part of my money and time is invested in it. In short, I'm entirely involved."

"Would I be prepared to engage fully in Business as Mission, including all the risks it would take?"

In time, the local business will operate independently and become financially profitable, with profits benefitting the local community. In the beginning stages, income is generated through professional workers delivering work to the firm in the Netherlands. Kees: "Meanwhile, help has come from unexpected sides, and we have seen God breaking down barriers in surrounding countries, enlarging the market for our services."

Crisis

The inner conviction to become fully engaged came at the end of a crisis period. Kees's business went through difficult times as a result of the financial crisis; at the same time, he was barely able to work because of a complicated heart surgery. "I was completely back to zero. I'm a go-go person, but this crisis made me sit still long enough to hear that voice in the dunes," shares Kees with a laugh, while continuing seriously: "May I add that you don't need to hear an audible voice; God is able to touch our hearts deeply in many ways."

"We work very hard, yet I am also relaxed. A wonderful peace originates from a deep trust that it does not depend on my efforts."

Being Available

Kees is not someone who spends a lot of time analyzing past experiences. In his view, the essence is *be obedient and be available*: be willing and ready to respond when God reveals something to you. The supernatural encounter and the following affirmation did give him extraordinary peace and energy. It also made him aware that he is not alone: "I'm convinced that this whole endeavor is God's work and initiative. That thought makes me feel unbeatable, as if I can walk right through a wall. We work very hard, yet I am also relaxed. A wonderful peace originates from a deep trust that it does not depend on my efforts. If I hadn't obeyed, God would have found someone else." Again, with his characteristic cheerful laugh, he says, "God knows a lot more people than I do!"

Kees's Partner: "We need to walk so close behind Jesus that we feel the dust of his slippers on our feet."

Walking "close behind Jesus" is a matter of life and death for John, his family, and his coworkers. It goes beyond a "nice spiritual aim." They live in an area where Christians can be killed for a supposed act of religious assertion—any day, any time. After John met his European partner Kees, they took two years of careful planning before they started their venture. His story resonates with depths of sacrifice, while showing glimpses of a miracle-working God. At the same time, it is a story of pragmatic and clearheaded thinking.

"We walk every day around the walls of our buildings," shares John, a gentle, engaging man in his mid-forties. "We check our walls for religiously provocative statements." This has happened to them a few times. It wasn't serious; some mischievous youth had done it, and it could be removed before anyone had noticed. But if a local jealous businessman turned against them, it could become serious: just ripping pages out of his Koran and throwing it in front of their door would mean great danger, since merely an accusation of religious hostility—true or not—can mean instant death. Besides such acts of jealousy or anger, it is also the desire of the followers of the mainstream Islamic faith to have "purity" in their area. Christians are identified with the West, and Westerners—for example— produce impure things like pornography. This country is known for a high percentage of pornography users, and secret tapes are for sale in many stores. While local men watch white Westerners on such videos, they conclude, "Those men and women do anything." For a variety of reasons, the lives of Christians—but also of followers of other faiths—are in danger. They are regarded by the mainstream as unholy, worthless, of no use.

Sons and Daughters of the Living King

To live and grow up in such surroundings has an effect on the local Christians. As Kees shared in the earlier story, their business has the aim to encourage and equip Christians to remain in Christ. "They have forgotten who they are: sons and daughters of the living king," says John, who studied and worked for a longer period in a Western context. "Next to the constant message of their fellow locals that they are worthless, the local Christian faith and worldview are influenced by an Islamic view of Jesus: a prophet, but not the one who rose from the dead and is part of the Triune God, the Son of the Maker of everything!"

"We want to empower [Christians] in the sense of enduring, growing, and flourishing—in the middle of these limitations."

"We want to empower Christians," continues John. "But not in the sense of bringing people out of poverty: from one level to a next level, because that next level will bring other, new concerns. We want to empower Christians while they live in the middle of constraints, in the middle of a lack of 'freedom,' the type of freedom where we can't sit or eat in the same room as others, where people with a PhD are considered worthless because of their religious identity. We want to empower in the sense of enduring, growing, and flourishing—in the middle of these limitations." John aims at serious discipleship: "When we aren't disciples—obeying and following Jesus—we are just members of a club and have become consumers." For John, following Jesus means walking behind him so closely that he can "feel the dust of his slippers" on his feet.

"When we aren't disciples—obeying and following Jesus—we are just members of a club and have become consumers."

John explains the local situation of the churches: "Local pastors are overburdened and too busy fielding threats to disciple their congregations. Besides being a pastor, they need to work. On top of that, their communities view them as their leaders. Christians don't go to the police or government but turn to their pastors for everything: when they are sick, out of work, or when a quarrel needs to be solved. Church members haven't learned to think and act for themselves."

Consumerism isn't just a Western problem. It just looks different in this particular Asian context, where people aren't used to taking responsibility because of their fear of unjust laws and exposure.
They hide behind their pastors and leaders for everything. Taking
personal responsibility to learn what it means to follow Jesus, and
the richness when they start doing so, is one aim of the discipleship
training. "The type of questions change when people go through our
discipleship program," shares John. "In the beginning, they asked
things like: 'How can I explain that we follow a Triune God?' but
the questions changed to 'How can I tell other people about following Jesus?'"

Begging

Setting up the institute, which is a step at a time turning into a
business, is a story of the impossible becoming possible. John was
told, "No one wants to work for a Christian company!" Finally, he
found a willing employee, and by the end of the first year everything
had changed drastically. "We have prayer and discussions with the
staff in the morning, but there was one worker who never said a
word. He was like a brick wall. But after a few months, he came into
my office and told me that all eighty-six workers of his former firm
had been fired for poor ethics and corruption. 'Can I thank God?
If I had stayed there, I would never have learned about truth and
I would have been in handcuffs myself now.' When he prayed, he
thanked God for his job and continued thanking God for much
more."

A year later, John no longer has trouble finding people willing
to work for him. On the contrary: "The word got around locally that
our organization cares for people and provides training of a high
international standard. Weekly, I get several requests; people are
even begging. They offer to get paid way less than they are earning
elsewhere."

Prayer Tool

John is familiar with a God who speaks and with following in
obedience, while experiencing the power of prayer and intercession.
This was deeply instilled in both him and his wife when God told

them to help someone in need during the time when they still lived in the West. "This person lost his mind while using drugs. We sent e-mails out and had five hundred people praying. God revealed to my wife the illusions this man was seeing due to the drugs, which he had come to believe. We made several trips to see him, and when the time was ripe my wife told him what God had revealed to her. He is totally restored to this day." At that time, John started thinking about developing a prayer tool to encourage more people to engage with the global church through prayer. For him, it's obviously not the latest Christian tech-thing, but he learned firsthand during the journey with Jesus—and in his present circumstances—that united prayer is a powerful and much-needed weapon in the heavenly realms.

Born in Asia, John and his wife lived and studied in the West. After his MBA studies, John received offers from major New York firms. They had the choice—staying in the US or returning to their home country—with the full realization of all the sacrifices this would involve. John shares, "We both told God that we would be available." Soon afterword, he met Kees. Both felt it was a God-ordained meeting. "We both agree that God is the head and the owner of this venue," says John. "God is our director."

"Take time to strategize . . . your venue needs to be able to survive you, way after your own death."

"We are an institution, gradually becoming a self-sustainable business. We slowly take steps to become a business and be self-reliant in this region. We view ourselves as a BAM business but do it differently than some other BAM businesses we know of." In closing, John gives this advice: "When starting a Business as Mission enterprise, take the time to think through how it will impact the generations to come. Take time to strategize, because to be able to really influence, your venue needs to be able to survive you, way after your own death."

CHAPTER 17

BUSINESS AS MISSION

Terminology and Content

By Mats Tunehag

In the future, I hope very few people will talk about Business as Mission. The term is like scaffolding: it is needed for a season as we build a new paradigm and praxis, businesses that glorify God and bring about holistic transformation of people and societies. The term "BAM" has its merits in clarification of the concept, and it has been helpful in the affirmation of businesspeople and the mobilization of resources. But the term itself is not important—the concept and the applications are.

In the general business world, there are also several terms for businesses that aim at multiple bottom lines serving multiple stakeholders. Some examples are social enterprise, creative capitalism, conscious capitalism, Corporate Social Responsibility, and inclusive business—different terms but with a similar concept.

Even this book highlights a limitation regarding terminology: In a world of about six thousand other languages, it is in English. We also acknowledge that BAM and other terms may not translate very well or at all into other languages. Thus the term is of secondary or tertiary importance. Terminology may vary in English and other languages, just as different BAM businesses have different public profiles. Some have a specific mission, such as fighting poverty or human trafficking. Others have a less specific niche, but they—like others—intentionally try to shape their businesses for God and the common good. We are not Christians merely doing social enterprise, however; God is always a stakeholder. He is the ultimate owner of our businesses. We want to see Christ manifested and God glorified through our businesses.

Despite the limitations of the terminology, what are some commonly agreed key ingredients of a BAM business? First, it is about business. Real business aimed at growing profitable and sustainable businesses. But we do business with a kingdom-of-God purpose and perspective. We pray and work toward a holistic transformation of people and societies. We believe that God can transform people and nations, and that businesses are strong transformational agents. BAM is authentic business, which aims at proclaiming, manifesting, and extending the kingdom of God. To that end, we plan, operate, and evaluate our businesses to make a positive impact economically, socially, environmentally, and spiritually. In this process, we recognize and value the stakeholders, not just the shareholders.

Business as Mission is a subset of the broader category of the theology of work and the theology of calling. Today, there is still a need to state the biblically obvious: God calls people to and equips people for business. Unfortunately, this is still a farfetched idea in many churches, mission conferences, and theological seminaries.

Mark Greene, executive director of the London Institute for Contemporary Christianity, has suggested that there are basically two strategies, two modus operandi, for the church: (1) We can try to get people to give some of their leisure time and spare money to church programs and mission activities; or (2) we can equip people for everyday work and activities, being salt and light to everyone in everything they do. Business as Mission is one expression of the second strategy: businesspeople being affirmed, equipped, and deployed to make a difference in the marketplace in and through business.

A paradigm shift takes time and often involves stress and pain. But once we have come through this, it becomes the assumed baseline. Until then, and throughout the shift, we need terms such as Business as Mission to highlight the inadequacies of the present paradigm and to guide us to a more biblical and holistic understanding of work, calling, and business.

Similar processes have happened before in the evangelical world, such as in 1974 when the Lausanne Congress focused on unreached peoples. Then, during the 1980s and 1990s, there was quite a bit of discussion on the term "unreached peoples." Some liked the term, while others questioned it. But it served well in clarifying a mission challenge and in mobilizing the church worldwide to develop strategies for unreached peoples. Today, there is less talk about the term "unreached peoples"—and less controversy—because it has indeed become a given. When a new paradigm and praxis have been established, the scaffolding can be removed.

Chris Dakas (Albania/The Balkans)
Engaging the Culture through Business

(Photo courtesy of Laura Dakas)

Chris Dakas was engaged in Business as Mission before anyone had heard of the term. Twenty-five years ago, he moved with his wife Laura to Tirana, the capital city of Albania. Together, they started the Stephen Center, which was the base for a restaurant/café, catering business, bed and breakfast, bakery, bookstore, printing shop, and radio station. Through these businesses, Chris has immersed himself into the local culture.

Although Chris Dakas encountered some hazards, he also gained major influence and was able with business profits to help start churches and social initiatives. His vision is to "create opportunities where the need is. It is about love and care."

"Owning your own restaurant is the dream of every Greek," says Chris, who grew up in a Greek community in the Boston area in the United States. He still remembers vividly how he loved to work in his uncle's restaurant as a young man. But at that time he didn't have the means to start his own place.

So, instead, he became a police officer.

Albania

His dream would become a reality many years later—in Albania of all places! After he retired early at a relatively young age (in his forties) from the police department, a whole other world opened up to him when he experienced a radical conversion around the same time. Chris and Laura then joined the Foursquare denomination and felt a call to missions in the country of Albania. This missionary "calling" happened in the 1990s, soon after the collapse of communism throughout the Soviet Bloc. Although Albania is constitutionally a secular country, about 70 percent of the 3.5 million Albanians consider themselves Muslim, while 30 percent see themselves as Christians, mainly Roman Catholic, Eastern Orthodox, or evangelical.

"We first wanted to be as close to Greece as possible," continues Chris. Chris's first thoughts were to open an English language school in a small village in the south of Albania. Even though they would have loved to live close to Greece, he quickly realized that his entrepreneurial spirit needed more space. Albania was just opening up and there were lots of needs, but also opportunities everywhere. Greek men were carrying refrigerators on their backs into Albania, selling them and going back the next day with another one. The village, however, was too small for Chris to seize the opportunities he saw, and he decided to settle in the capital city of Tirana.

In Tirana, Chris thrived with his gift of seeing opportunities as well as creating them. In the city center, he acquired a plot of land with a building where he realized his dream of establishing a restaurant. The Stephen Center (http://www.stephencenter.com) was known early on to be the best restaurant in town because of the food and excellent service, and it continues to have a good reputation. "We train our employees to really care for people," says Chris. "Training Albanians with a communist background to give good service is a challenge, but we consider training them professionally as a part of our mission."

The Stephen Center restaurant became the backbone for all kinds of initiatives, some of which were related (like the bakery, catering, and bed and breakfast), as well as some that were not (a bookstore and printing shop). Some of their patrons were government officials, as the Stephen Center owned one of the first printing shops in town. Meanwhile, a popular radio station was started in another part of the country, which serves people from all walks of life, offering a Christian message that is aired regularly.

Besides being an entrepreneur, Chris is an evangelist with a gift of generosity, wanting to help whomever and wherever possible. For example, over the years he has helped to establish and support five Foursquare Churches in different parts of the country, as well as a church in Kosovo.

Wild West

Opportunities came their way, but also with a number of difficulties. They were able to obtain the building from an Austrian lady who they discovered was the widow of an Albanian man who belonged to a notorious family. This family—to express it mildly—didn't take the law seriously. The lady preferred to sell her property to Chris, but the family wasn't pleased with her decision. As a result, Chris and Laura were harassed for years with threats and slander. It was like "Albanian Wild West times." However, with his background as a police officer, Chris wasn't easily intimidated.

Influence

The restaurant and also some of the other business ventures were a way to connect with influential people and a door to various opportunities that proved to be a blessing. Members of the government and the American Embassy visit regularly. "The present city mayor is one of my very good friends," says Chris.

During the Kosovo War (1998–99), the United Nations asked Chris to oversee and manage four refugee camps. At the height of the conflict, over four thousand people sought refuge in Albania. "The UN considered me as a local whom they could trust."

Refugees

Today, Chris is involved with the Syrian refugee crisis in Greece. Through activating his business connections, he has been able to provide warm and dry shelter for pregnant women close to giving birth. He is renting a building with apartments to be used for the refugee families.

Another project is giving tens of thousands of SD cards for mobile phones so refugees can read, hear, and see the gospel in their own language. At this point, not many refugees have entered Albania because of little prospects and difficult border crossing. Chris, however, is still expecting and preparing for refugees. It is part of his mantra: "Go where the need is. Love people, and do something you love doing."

CHAPTER 18

WALL STREET VERSUS BAM STREET

By Mats Tunehag

Return on investment: ROI. This is a common term and acronym in the financial world, as well as in the business community. People invest in businesses with a hope of getting a good return. This is also the lifeblood of the stock exchanges around the world. Companies need financial capital to start and to grow. Many startups obtain money from the three Fs: friends, family, and fools. They may never see their money grow or return.

We acknowledge the importance of both financial capital and investors, but we also need to review the concept of ROI. The most prevalent paradigm is a Wall Street concept. Simply put, Wall Street is relatively one-dimensional: it is about money. Investors put some money into a business, with the hope and expectation to get more money back in the shortest time possible. It is a two-way street: money goes from investor to business, and then back from business to investor. This is not bad or evil, but we need to think bigger, beyond the traditional ROI. We need to move from Wall Street to BAM Street.[1]

Business as Mission is about seeking a positive impact on multiple bottom lines for multiple stakeholders through business. In BAM, God is always one of the stakeholders, thus we are not Christians just doing social enterprise. BAM Street is different from Wall Street. A company needs financial capital and it needs to make a

---

1. As the Wall Street model is too limited, we need a broader and more impactful BAM Street concept. See Mats' two-minute video, "BAM Street," at: https://mats'/vimeo.com/152713984.

profit, but that's not all. We recognize the importance of other bottom lines as well. John Mackey, founder of Whole Foods, states that businesses should "endeavor to create financial, intellectual, social, cultural, emotional, spiritual, physical, and ecological wealth for all their stakeholders."[2] Likewise, BAM Street recognizes the importance of investors, business owners, and operators, but it also values other stakeholders such as employees, customers, suppliers, family, church, community, environment, and ultimately, God.

BAM Street is multidimensional. Besides financial capital, we are intentional about putting other kinds of capital into a business: intellectual capital (for example, through mentoring) and spiritual input (for instance, prayer). BAM Street is more of a roundabout which has multiple entry and exit points, rather than a simple two-way street. I may put money into a BAM business, but the financial return (part or whole) may go to some other entity in the BAM ecosystem. Part of the profit can go the community, to profit-sharing schemes, or to investments in other BAM companies. BAM Street engages people and groups with diverse resources to use business as a blessing on many levels and for many stakeholders.[3] BAM Street engages more people and groups with various resources to use business as a means to bless many stakeholders at multiple levels.[4]

The global BAM movement needs more financial capital. But more money is not enough if we still think and operate with a Wall Street concept. We also need a discussion of how we define ROI. Should we settle for Wall Street, or should we move toward the more holistic BAM Street approach? With the latter model, we can see more and different kinds of capital invested in businesses, and with more returns to more stakeholders.

---

2. John Mackey and Raj Sisodia, *Conscious Capitalism: Liberating the Heroic Spirit of Business* (Cambridge, MA: Harvard Business Review, 2014).

3. To learn more about how a BAM Street model has been working since 2001, see http://www.transformationalsme.org.

4. Justin Welby, the archbishop of Canterbury, writes: "Inclusive capitalism does not always seek the maximisation of reward, but rather the maximisation of human flourishing." Justin Welby, "Capitalism should stop being so self-serving," *The Telegraph* (June 25, 2015), http://www.telegraph.co.uk/news/religion/11696974/Capitalism-should-stop-being-so-self-serving.html.

Chuck Welden and Mark Wesson (Birmingham, Alabama)

*Real Businesses Competing for Real
Investors to Make Real Impact*

Mark Wesson and Chuck Welden. (Photo
courtesy of the ones interviewed)

*Business as Mission companies should be commercial high-impact
firms that are intentional in creating wealth socially, spiritually, and
financially. That is what Chuck Welden and Mark Wesson believe.
Along with others in Birmingham, Alabama, they initiated the Lion's
Den to provide such businesses a stage, while attracting investors and
high-profile businesspeople. Their model is now spreading to other
cities, countries, and continents.*

In 2014 in Birmingham, Alabama, the Lion's Den (http://www
.thelionsden.us) began with the aim to inspire, educate, and mobi-
lize Christian businesspeople. By offering a professional and enter-
taining program, they have created "a place to be" and an "on-ramp"
for Business as Mission. Within three years, over a thousand people
from over twenty-five states and ten countries have attended the
annual event. While most attendees are business professionals, students, and academics, ministry and NGO leaders also participate.
Surrounding the event is a keynote luncheon and a professional
summit that focuses on Business as Mission.

Presenters

Presenters can be conducting business anywhere in the world. Each year, four businesses chosen from over twenty applicants present their business plan, which includes an overview of their quadruple bottom line and how they aim to be successful in the four areas: social, spiritual, environmental, and financial. Before they enter the stage, a three-minute video provides a context for their business: why they became involved, where the business is located, and how their initiative benefits society and advances the kingdom, while being profitable. Following this video, each presenter gives an eight-minute presentation, after which a panel of six "Lions" asks questions and challenges them on their assumptions and projections. Presenters have ranged from a ferry service in East Africa to the movie *Woodlawn* to innovative medical devices to hydroelectricity in Rwanda to a cattle feed lot in Ethiopia.

The Lion's Den is presented by Cedarworks, Inc., while Samford University in Birmingham hosts the event. The involvement of this Christian university is beneficial for both parties. "We saw the advantage of being associated with a respected entity," says Mark. "Samford's aim is to help their students integrate Christian faith in the workplace, and our event provides good examples for their students and faculty to see business success coupled with gospel outreach. Both of us see the importance of impacting the next generation."

The concept is spreading like wildfire. Christian businesspeople from places such as Dallas, Memphis, Nashville, and Minneapolis have come to Birmingham to ask advice regarding the possibility of putting on a Lion's Den in their cities. Samford University wrote about the event in their newsletter, and an alumnus working in Uganda with refugees took note. Since he is looking for more sustainable ways to give aid, he contacted the Birmingham team to investigate how to host an event in Africa.

Edutainment

"We surf on the success of the TV series the *Shark Tank*," admits Mark. "This reality show has millions of fans." In this show, entrepreneurial contestants make business presentations to a panel of "shark" investors, who then choose whether or not to invest. Though the

Lion's Den has a similar format, its focus is a mixture of education and entertainment to produce "edutainment." "But it's not all fun and games," adds Mark. "A number of qualified investors are in the audience, and many of them follow up with the presenters to discuss the possibility of investing in their company."

An important ingredient to the Lion's Den success is that Birmingham, at just over a million people, is still a relatively small city in a relational sense. Both Chuck and Mark are well known in the local business community. Chuck's family is active in real estate, and Mark in finance and banking. Chuck explains: "In the South, barbecue, college football, church, and hunting provide a lot of face time. Having this type of regular interface accelerates trust, allows for accountability, and stimulates new ideas and purpose regarding BAM. Without a strong bond, there is not sufficient trust to move forward; if needed, we can call our group together within forty-eight hours."

Overwhelmed by Response

The core group consists of about twenty people. "It is important for any group to include a myriad of people at different stages of life and with different resources," says Mark. "Some of us are more visionary, others have time or resources to give, and some simply want an assignment they can work on, while others may have a broader network available to draw on where they can use their affluence and influence." They were able to successfully draw others into BAM because of "gravitas," adds Mark. "I'm quoting one of our members who credits the Lion's Den success largely to our core members who have proven long-term professional success, demonstrated capacity to invest at an impactful scale, have an understanding of BAM based on experience, travel, and relationships, and have the ability to pull people together."

Captured by the BAM Concept

"Nothing flourishes by itself," notes Mark, emphasizing the need to build a team. Chuck and Mark were independently looking for a way to have missional impact beyond writing a check or building a school on a typical missions trip to the developing world. They both wanted to discover a way to use their business skills in mission. Chuck first heard about the BAM concept in 2002 when he tracked down Tom Sudyk and Jeri Little, both pioneers in Business as Mission in India and Romania. Chuck shares: "Mark and I started meeting every three to six months. God brought us others looking for the same thing, and all of a sudden we were with fifteen people meeting once a month. It was a manageable size group, and we are all headed in the same direction. It allowed for relationship building and development of vision, mission, and strategy."

Chuck and Mark had previously never thought about their business being a BAM business; subconsciously, they had segmented their lives into "business/work" and "church/mission." Chuck says, "We knew our work was important and sharing faith was a normal thing to do. We'd give money, as the donor driven model was prevalent, but it created a lack of fulfillment." Something seemed to be missing. "We were looking for something more robust, a greater use of our skills. Somehow we thought mission was solely about building hospitals and evangelization."

> *"The donor driven model was prevalent, but
> it created a lack of fulfillment."*

During a mission trip with his daughter to evangelize Thai students, Chuck began a serious search. It started during a soccer game with the students: "I wasn't fit, and felt like a fool playing with these young college athletes. I kept wondering if there were other ways to be involved in missions, while using my God-given entrepreneur skills."

Chuck got help from one of these students, who did an internship with him. Part of this student's assignment was to help Chuck find ways to use his business skills in mission. "I wanted to use something other than my back, pocketbook, or mediocre knowledge of other languages." The assignment led to the BAM pioneers in India and Romania. When Mark and Chuck discovered that those stories had been featured in the *New York Times* in an article on Business as Mission, they knew they were on the right track.

Even though things stayed low profile in Birmingham for years, they always knew they had to be prepared to "go public" and are at times still surprised by how much the BAM message has resonated with fellow businesspeople. More people showed up and became more excited than expected, which brought along another challenge: "When there is delay between inspiration and implementation, it can lead to frustration," says Chuck. So they started identifying various ways people could get involved, depending on gifts, talents, and resources. Some of those were: mentoring, coaching, incubating, going on vision trips, moving overseas to work at a BAM business, helping with events, or identifying companies that have overseas operations but never thought how their business could advance the gospel. They even came up with a name for this: "on-ramps."

Connect, Inspire, Educate, Mobilize

"We don't want people to just get excited about BAM. We want to help them into the game," emphasizes Chuck. The Birmingham network list has grown to eight hundred people, while the yearly event includes hundreds of people with qualified investors investing substantial funds in Business as Mission companies—with the intent of reaping a healthy return and enabling these companies to achieve success in their quadruple bottom lines.

Participating in a Global Movement

Both men, and other members of the team, are passionate about using their time, treasures, and talents to help the BAM movement forward. Connecting, inspiring, educating, and mobilizing regarding BAM is done locally at the Lion's Den events, but also globally year-round. Part of their job is to visit and research businesses on other continents. "We enjoy being around businesspeople," shares Mark. "When there, meeting businesspeople in China or Israel, we find that we talk the same language since we share similar struggles. Once you broach the topic, everyone quickly concludes they want to use their business skills to make an impact."

Their travels have brought them in contact with key leaders within the BAM movement, who in turn have supported their work in Birmingham. Chuck and Mark are encouraged by what they see. Chuck: "Worldwide great groups are engaged with BAM. It shows a greater ecosystem; others are also advancing the ball. It is our prayer that we will be a small part of a global solution, which is turning into a global movement."

CHAPTER 19

BUSINESS AS MISSION AND HUMAN TRAFFICKING

By Mats Tunehag

In the 1700s, the slave trade was widely accepted and legal. It was, in fact, the backbone of the British Empire's economy. It was a large, organized, and transnational business. Then William Wilberforce and the Clapham group decided to fight this evil trade. They chose to attack the systemic issue—the legality of the slave trade and slavery. To that end, they organized a decades-long campaign focusing on justice, aiming at a root cause. They worked politically to change unjust and ungodly laws that permitted this dehumanizing trade. They could have chosen an easier route of awareness campaigns and a boycott of sugar from plantations in Jamaica, but they knew that such initiatives in and of themselves would not free the slaves or bring about lasting change.

Charity and Justice

Today, although the slave trade and slavery are illegal, they are not dead. Just like Wilberforce and his colleagues, we need to ask what the systemic issue is today, and we need to go beyond charitable actions to fight for justice.

In early 2016, my wife, Jennifer, and I visited Saint Andrew Catholic Church in Clemson, South Carolina. Their vision statement struck us:

> "Charity" is the generosity that alleviates needs that are immediate. "Justice" is the process by which generosity configures our ways of providing education, delivering health care, doing business, and creating

laws that lessen the need for charity. There will always be immediate needs even in the most just of worlds.

> Charity is the more attractive generosity. We see immediate results for the better and we enjoy—here and now—the gratification that comes from doing good. Justice is less attractive because it usually calls for personal and communal change, and we are creatures of habit.[1]

A Root Cause of Human Trafficking

We need to identify the root causes of human trafficking. One answer is unemployment. Places with high unemployment and underemployment become high-risk areas where traffickers trick and trap vulnerable people looking for jobs. Thus we cannot talk about adequate prevention of human trafficking unless we include the need for jobs with dignity.[2]

We must also answer the question: Out of trafficking and into what? Jobs with dignity provide survivors with a hope for sustainable freedom. So, effective prevention *and* restoration require jobs. Who can create jobs with dignity? Businesspeople.

Business Solutions: BAM and Freedom Businesses

In 2012, the Business as Mission Global Think Tank assigned a working group to explore business solutions to human trafficking. The group identified businesses that aim at providing solutions to human trafficking, particularly by providing jobs for prevention and restoration.[3]

Called "freedom businesses," they exist to fight human trafficking. There are several types of businesses that fit into this category. Businesses that create jobs for survivors of exploitation would be the most familiar. Other workplaces hire vulnerable people in order to

---

1. Find out more about the vision of the Saint Andrew Catholic Church at http://www.saclemson.org/a-parish-vision.

2. In 2015, Mats wrote a longer article on this subject of human trafficking, a root cause, and business solutions. See http://matstunehag.com/2015/05/17/human-trafficking-and-freedom-through-enterprise.

3. For more on the development of the Freedom Business Alliance, see Jennifer Tunehag's interview at http://businessasmission.com/fba-interview.

prevent exploitation, or aggregate products from these first two and bring them to new markets. Because employment is an important aspect of human dignity, freedom businesses offer opportunities to people whose main qualification is the need for a job.[4]

Freedom Business Alliance

In October 2013, the BAM Global Think Tank produced a groundbreaking report, *A Business Takeover: Combating the Business of the Sex Trade with Business as Mission*.[5]

This report catalyzed the launch of the Freedom Business Alliance (FBA),[6] a global trade association that believes business can be a powerful tool in the holistic restoration of individuals and the transformation of their communities. FBA exists to help freedom businesses succeed by providing business training and mentoring, industry research, networking opportunities, information, resources, and marketplace connections.

---

4. See Jennifer Tunehag's introduction to freedom businesses at https://vimeo.com/152460926.

5. Jo Plummer and Mats Tunehag, eds., "A Business Takeover: Combating the Business of the Sex Trade with Business as Mission," *Report by the Business as Mission Think Tank Group: Business as Mission and Human Trafficking* (BAM Global Think Tank, October 2013), http://bamglobal.org/report-trafficking.

6. See the FBA introductory video at http://www.freedombusinessalliance.com.

Ryan and Andrea Crozier (Romania)

Empowering Locals to Battle Injustice

Ryan and Andrea Crozier (back row, far right)
with team members of eLiberare.

American Ryan Crozier has been working to help raise awareness around human trafficking in Romania. "There are more slaves today than ever before. God is the Defender of the poor. He gets angry about injustice." Ryan identifies with this character trait of the living God and went to Romania to help battle social injustice. To be able to do so, this American entrepreneur started an association and, through a twist of fate, also a business. Both grew exponentially in just a few years. Some key factors contributed to the success.

In 2012, Ryan and Andrea Crozier arrived in Romania, and within a year they had started the association eLiberare (http://www.eliberare.com/en/), with the aim of raising awareness about the problem of human trafficking within Romania. The UN lists this country as a main source within Europe of human trafficking. But up to a few years ago, Romanians themselves were hardly aware that this problem existed. Through this lack of awareness, vulnerable people were even more prone to believe false promises of "a better life elsewhere." Within three years, eLiberare and its message have become well known nationwide, and its Facebook page now has twenty thousand followers. Schoolteachers from different parts of the country know of this organization, and they are working to inform their students of the dangers of human trafficking. Government leaders have invited eLiberare to participate in discussions on this problem. Meanwhile, churches—which used to stay away from this issue since it was sex related—have started to cooperate and bring attention in their services to this problem. Ryan shares, "We focused on education, government, and church to bring awareness in the country. Our name helped: eLiberare means being free and liberated. We can all identify with being free human beings."

Success Factors

The success in raising awareness is not just due to choosing a good name or to creativity in communication. There are other reasons why an American is welcomed at the table by Romanian government organizations, NGOs, schools, and churches. Ryan and Andrea are serious about developing relationships with Romanians, with the aim to serve. One way they do so is by partnering and collaborating, while giving "honor away" by first mentioning names of Romanian partners while downplaying eLiberare's role. "We want to help local people to address these issues," explains Ryan. "In communist times, the government solved the problems. After the wall fell, many NGOs and foreigners came. But as foreigners we must realize that Romanians themselves have the most potential to influence society. We are here to empower them and serve alongside."

The Business

Another factor contributing to their influence is that eLiberare itself develops and creates materials that they give away for free. This is made possible through a business Ryan started, Agency Boon (https://www.agencyboon.com), which is an outsourced team of skilled Romanians hired by creative agencies worldwide. Services they offer range from assistance with brand identity and web design to motion graphics, illustrations, and editing. "We serve as an extension of their own creative teams," explains Ryan. "The profit is good because of lower labor costs here in Romania, and we don't have the hassle of recruiting and dealing with clients. All profits go 100 percent to charities in Romania, which is an extra motivation for agencies to hire our team."

"By becoming a business, doors opened more easily, also because we came to the table with something to offer."

A business was not part of Ryan's initial plans; but when funding didn't come through, he saw an opportunity and jumped into it. He had creative and skilled people among his staff, as well as connections with a creative agency. Their first project was small, but within four years the business had grown to a yearly turnover of $300,000.

Being self-supportive was another reason why doors opened up for Ryan and his staff: "In Western society, NGOs are respected, but not so in Romania. Here, business is more respected. By becoming a business, doors opened more easily also, because we came to the table with something to offer."

Developing a Business to Start and Fund More Charities

Looking back, though, Ryan would have done things differently. "There is a tension between the focus on battling human trafficking and managing a growing business like Agency Boon. At first all we did was interwoven; we needed to sort things out and bring clarity." Meanwhile, Ryan has given over eLiberare into the hands of a capable Romanian staff, and he now focuses on growing another business with the aim to start and fund more charities. "I need to start something new every couple of years," Ryan admits. "We've just started partnering with a young woman, who is starting a community development project with a focus of helping youth in our neighborhood. I can see that developing into another charity. I support that strongly, because I believe that we as Christians need to become more involved with the needs of our society. Strengthening local communities is another way to battle human trafficking."

Love for Romania

Ryan knew from a young age that his future would be in Romania. His love for this country runs deep and has a history, as he bonded at a young age with Romanians. In 1997, when he was twelve years old, his father took him along on a mission trip to Bucharest to work among street kids. That trip was life changing for him and his family: "Kids my age were living in the sewage system of Bucharest. I saw them sniffing glue and selling their bodies to survive. Some girls would dress as boys to try to prevent sexual abuse. It impacted me deeply."

In the following years, Ryan and his parents made many visits to Romania. They spent time in Bucharest while helping different ministries. "We participated in their lives and got to know the people. We have found many people who have blessed us richly with hospitality and generosity."

> *"I discuss all my major decisions with him, and
> I won't go ahead if he doesn't agree."*

Living and working among the Romanians with his parents in his teenage years set an example. It also contributed to his present success, because when Ryan and Andrea came to start a ministry it was natural for them to have a learning attitude. One of the staff members of a ministry he knew when he was a teenage boy is now the leader of Teen Challenge Romania. Ryan: "He is my best friend, counselor, and safe place here in Romania. I discuss all my major decisions with him, and I won't go ahead if he doesn't agree."

As Ryan looks back over his past accomplishments, he mentions another key: Just before coming to Romania, he had a divine encounter. Even though he doesn't experience mountaintop victorious faith all the time, those first years in Romania were extraordinary. His encounter with God during a two-day retreat gave him insights into certain parts of God's character, which strengthened his own identity. "It was a monumental experience. I knew I was a child of God, a mighty warrior, a light in darkness, a defender of the poor, a lover of joy, and a broken vessel. Once in Romania, I just knew I would have favor and was indeed surrounded by yes! Andrea and I love being here," Ryan concludes. "I want to be buried here. My hope is to be a small part of seeing the church in Romania rise up and engage their community in a way that leaves a lasting impact on society."

CHAPTER 20

BUSINESS AS MISSION

A Modern Movement with Historical Roots and a Global Scope

By Mats Tunehag

It is natural and easy to focus on our lifetime and on our immediate geographical context. But as Christians we need to stand at the crossroads of history and the whole world. History is *his story*. There is a metanarrative of creation, fall, and redemption, and it has a global perspective—"for God so loved the world."

BAM Has Roots and a History

We mustn't forget or cut off our roots. Remember that Jesus was a Jew and Martin Luther was a Catholic. Although there is a strong engagement by evangelicals in the BAM movement, BAM is not limited to this group. Theologically, conceptually, historically, and practically, BAM is not confined to a particular denomination. BAM is ultimately rooted in who God is and who we are, as created in his image.

Through the Holy Scriptures, we learn about the sanctity of work and the gift and command of wealth creation. We can read of God-fearing people doing business with a positive impact on people and communities.

Throughout history—and around the globe—there are examples of people shaping businesses for God and the common good. The BAM movement is a part of this, a continuation. But we have a responsibility in our day and age to be rooted in Scripture and history and to connect with others nationally, regionally, and globally, as we do business unto the Lord and serve people. As Pope John Paul II wrote:

> [For] the lay faithful have the responsibility of being in the forefront in working out a solution to the very serious problems of growing unemployment . . . to raise up new forms of entrepreneurship and to look again at systems of commerce, finance and exchange of technology.[1]

Or, as we saw earlier, Pope Francis has more recently stated:

> Business is a noble vocation, directed to producing wealth and improving the world. It can be a fruitful source of prosperity for the area in which it operates, especially if it sees the creation of jobs as an essential part of its service to the common good.[2]

BAM Is Bigger Than BAM

Although "Business as Mission" is a term in English, the movement is bigger than the term and it is not limited to English. If you do an Internet search on "Business as Mission," you will find a lot of sources, but these won't give you a fair picture of the global and diverse nature of the BAM movement. It will only give you a picture of BAM initiatives that use English—and there are six thousand other languages in the world! The Internet displays only the BAM initiatives that have chosen to go public and market themselves.

For example, two of the bigger BAM initiatives in the world operate in Korean[3] and Bahasa. BAM also speaks Chinese, and there is a Hong Kong-based BAM organization that has published a lot of BAM material in Chinese, both old and simplified script.[4] Another indicator of the international scope of BAM is that BAM material is available in at least nineteen different languages: Arabic, Bahasa, Chinese, Dutch, English, Farsi, Finnish, French, German, Greek,

---

1. *Post-Synodal Apostolic Exhortation* Christifideles Laici *of His Holiness John Paul II on the Vocation and the Mission of the Lay Faithful in the Church and in the World* (December 30, 1988).
2. Pope Francis, *Encyclical Letter* Laudato Si', #29.
3. See http://matstunehag.com/wp-content/uploads/2011/04/BAM-IBA-Movements-with-a-rich-history-and-a-bright-future-v-15-May.pdf.
4. See www.chinesebam.com.

Japanese, Korean, Polish, Portuguese, Russian, Spanish, Swedish, Turkish, and Vietnamese.[5]

BAM: The Movement

Twenty years ago, we could not have credibly talked about a global BAM movement. Today, by the grace of God, we can. The first global think tank on BAM (2003–4) and the Lausanne paper on BAM (2004)[6] helped catalyze a common global understanding of the concept. It sought to address how businesses can:

- serve people
- align with God's purposes
- be good stewards of the planet and
- make a profit

This is often referred to as the quadruple bottom line. We aim at a positive impact economically, socially, environmentally, and spiritually, which will lead to the holistic transformation of people and societies—to the greater glory of God. We are especially concerned about the world's poorest and least evangelized peoples.

The second global think tank process (2011–13) increased connections, which in turn created a global connectivity of key players in the BAM ecosystem with people from every continent. This BAM think tank had approximately thirty national, regional, and international working groups collaborating. Leaders from these groups and other BAM leaders at large, about eighty in total, met at the Leaders' Forum in April 2013 in Thailand.

Following this forum, we saw the largest global gathering of social and intellectual capital in the BAM space. More than five hundred and fifty people from over forty nations came to the BAM Congress later in the month. The congress collaborated with a BAM Trade Fair, which followed immediately after and had over two hundred participants.

---

5. See http://matstunehag.com/bam-material-in-different-languages.
6. See http://www.matstunehag.com/wp-content/uploads/2011/04/BAM-LOP-June-05.pdf.

These BAM think tanks, processes, meetings, and reports, as well as the BAM Congress, have been instrumental in building a global BAM movement, establishing a shared vision, developing common values, and facilitating a global network of BAM practitioners and other key leaders in the overall BAM ecosystem.[7]

Today, BAM Global[8] continues to serve. We exist to invigorate the global BAM movement by facilitating communication and collaboration among four major constituencies: leaders in business, church, mission, and academia. All four of these groups have been engaged in the think tanks, the BAM Global Congress, various national and regional consultations, and in the Think Tank reports.[9] But the BAM movement continues to grow in size, range, and impact, and it is bigger than BAM Global.

Wealth Creation

In March 2017, the Lausanne Movement and BAM Global organized a Global Consultation on the Role of Wealth Creation for Holistic Transformation in Chiang Mai, Thailand. About thirty people from twenty nations participated, primarily from the business world but also from the church, missions, and academia.

During the consultation process between 2016 and 2017, we discussed various aspects of wealth creation, including justice, poverty, biblical foundation, wealth creators, stewardship of creation, and the role of the church. Between August and December 2017, we published the findings in seven papers and produced an educational video. A book will be published as well. The Wealth Creation Manifesto conveys the essentials of our deliberations before and during the consultation. It is already available in thirteen languages and is being translated into more.[10]

To read the manifesto and learn more about the background and global deliberations on this topic over the years, see the appendices of this book, "Wealth Creation Manifesto" and "Consultation on Wealth Creation: Background and Context."

---

7. See also http://businessasmission.com.
8. See http://bamglobal.org.
9. As of February 2017, BAM Global has published nineteen reports. You can read them at http://bamglobal.org/reports.
10. See http://matstunehag.com/wealth-creation/.

BAM Global Congress

The first BAM Global Congress in 2013 was a landmark gathering for the BAM movement worldwide. Part of its appeal was a unique opportunity to bring together our BAM community from all regions and around a broad range of topics and issues. The second BAM Global Congress will take place in 2020 in Southeast Asia and will provide a connecting point for the global BAM community.

Sam Cho (South Korea)

Learning from the South Korean BAM Movement

(Photo courtesy of Sam Cho)

Sam Cho is convinced that Business as Mission has something to say to every Christian: "The global culture is capitalism; as a result, all of us are living and working in a business culture. How are we being salt and light and living out God's principles in that culture?" This Canadian Korean business professor advocates for BAM within the broader Korean Church, especially in China and South Korea, but also in other parts of the world.

"BAM is one of God's initiatives to get Christians active in the marketplace," Sam Cho believes. "We are called to be active in the public space. In Jesus' time, Christians were active in the public space within Roman culture; now we live in a globalized world with mass migration to urban centers where capitalism is the main paradigm. God is challenging us to think through how we are going to live out kingdom values in our present global business culture."

Missional Movement

In South Korea, mission agencies have worked together to set up IBA, the International BAM Alliance (http://www.iba-all.org), to develop various initiatives. One of those is Neo Moravian House, a one-month full-time summer school for missionaries where they can learn how to do Business as Mission. "Missionaries who want to do BAM need business skills," explains Sam. "Their whole mind-set about mission needs to be transformed. This month is at least required to accomplish this."

Sam grew up in Canada, served internationally, and is now the director of the international mission agency Interserve Korea. To Sam, however, BAM is not just for missionaries: "The BAM perspective is about missional life in real-life context. For that reason we developed with colleagues the Center for BAM (www.centerforBAM .com) to educate Korean Christians in the business world how to live missionally." They have done this through an online platform over the past several years in order to disseminate the idea of missional life for all Christians through the BAM movement. "This training is not just for entrepreneurs. We invite all laymen and women, since all of us live in a business culture."

The Protestant churches in Korea are mission minded, and BAM as a way to be involved in mission is appealing to South Koreans. Two hundred years ago, the Catholics introduced Christianity, but it is the Protestant missionaries who came a hundred years later who are especially revered in the South Korean memory. Through the missionaries' commitment in bringing the gospel in a dark period in Korean history under Japanese oppression, about 20 percent of the population became Protestant and managed to develop themselves in different areas. With this positive change still fresh in mind, Korean Christians value foreign mission and are often eager to participate.

Sam grew up in Canada and was himself a missionary in China and North Korea from 2000 to 2010. During that period, he had already connected with the mission organization Interserve and worked as a business professor at a Christian university established by South Koreans. While there, Sam developed with colleagues a BAM incubating group, supporting business initiatives through funding and advising. They helped young Chinese launch businesses such as coffee shops, which supported poor local churches; a business consulting company; an online business for handicapped people; and a business with a focus on architecture and city development.

Global Korean BAM Movement

Both in and outside South Korea, Business as Mission is becoming a missional movement among Koreans. Next to Koreans valuing foreign missions, the ones in the Korean diaspora are often involved in business. An example is a church in Shanghai, China, which is attended by three thousand South Koreans, many of whom are expatriates and in some way involved in the business world. In 2007, this church started yearly well-attended Business as Mission conferences, which Sam was asked to organize in Shanghai. In addition, Sam is involved in yearly Korean BAM gatherings held in Seoul, New York, and Australia.

A Paradigm Shift Is Needed

The yearly BAM conference organized by IBA in South Korea attracts hundreds of people. Despite the interest and growth, Sam experiences resistance and misunderstanding. "A paradigm shift is needed in the churches," he explains. "In Korea, as well as in North America, it is all about church planting and church growth. Christians are encouraged to run away from the world into 'holy land,' where they are taught to be good Christians and to be active in the church; but we need to repent from our dualism. We need to be active in the world, not just in the church. We need to live the gospel in the world operated by a business culture. There we need to be light in the darkness."

> *"We should not accept the business culture and capitalism as it is. . . . We need to ask ourselves what God has to say about consumerism, production, and investment."*

Sam and his colleagues are thinking through what this means as they feel that Business as Mission is not just about how to set up a Christian company, but that it is much more fundamental. They aim to develop countercultural kingdom values through questioning the present paradigms. "We should not accept the business culture and capitalism as it is. Some of it is good, but a lot is not. We need to ask ourselves what God has to say about consumerism, production, and investment. How do we consume; what is our motive when buying goods? Do we need the product, and do we realize how it was made? Besides the way we consume, we need to ask ourselves what and how we are producing. Is the product good for the environment and for the people? Are there other ways to create value through creativity and hard work? In the area of investing money and time, we also need to question present practices."

---

*"Redemption starts with our daily activities.
All of us are involved."*

"The overall question is if we redeem business," continues Sam. "When a Christian company just goes along with the flow and doesn't show a difference in these issues, we disgrace the gospel even more. As a BAM movement, we need to reflect God's character of justice, fairness, and love in all activities. Redemption starts with our daily activities." Sam concludes: "All of us are involved."

CHAPTER 21

BUSINESS AS MISSION AND THE OLIVE TREE

Throughout history, there have been movements of societal transformation. Key leaders—such as Luther, Calvin, Knox, and Zwingli—catalyzed the Protestant Reformation. Approximately two hundred years ago, William Wilberforce and others led the movement to abolish slavery and the slave trade. In the 1960s, Martin Luther King Jr. and the civil rights movement fought for significant change in the United States.

Societal transformation implies good and lasting transformation. It is not about achieving perfection—there will always be room for improvement. On the other hand, societal transformation can also be bad, such as in Europe in the 1930s and '40s, which ended with the Holocaust, or as seen in the negative consequences of the Islamic revolution in Iran from 1979 onward.

Looking at the movements—for good—of societal transformation, we can observe some common themes and denominators:

- They started as a small minority.
- They shared a vision.
- They embraced common values.
- They connected with one another.
- They built critical mass.
- They had commendable tenacity.

Business as Mission is another movement for societal transformation. Today, there is a global BAM movement, which was not the case twenty years ago. Although there were expressions of BAM back then and even long before that, now there is an unprecedented global cohesion and connectedness.

Doing BAM to achieve societal transformation is not like instant coffee: take a few bits of BAM thinking, stir them into a businss and—voilà!—transformation. No, societal transformation takes time. We want to set a stage and serve our generation in such a way that it will be a blessing for many generations to come.

We can learn from the olive tree. Many of us think in terms of two kinds of olives: green or black. But there are a thousand or more varieties! In the BAM movement, we are not just two categories: businesspeople on the one hand, and church and mission people on the other. Instead, we are part of a greater ecosystem of investors, bookkeepers, prayer partners, entrepreneurs, academics, human trafficking experts, theologians, marketing and salespeople, and many others.

After planting an olive tree, it takes about twenty-five years before it bears edible fruit. But once it starts bearing fruit, it can produce olives for two thousand years or more! Olive trees are intergenerational blessings.

The modern BAM movement is still young, and we are in some ways still within the first twenty-five years of the life of an olive tree. We do see some fruit, but we eagerly await more. In this stage of growth, the BAM olive tree needs care and feeding; it needs the strategic and intentional investment of time and resources.

We want to build a movement that can bring the good and lasting "fruit" of transformation, which we know will take time. In the meantime, we hold tenaciously to our vision as we further develop and grow BAM businesses. We embrace the promise that God will bless us so that we can be a blessing—in and through business—in our generation and for many generations to come. And to that end, as we state in the 2004 "Business as Mission Manifesto":

> We call upon the Church worldwide to identify, affirm, pray for, commission and release businesspeople and entrepreneurs to exercise their gifts and calling as businesspeople in the world—among all peoples and to the ends of the earth.
>
> We call upon businesspeople globally to receive this affirmation and to consider how their gifts and experience might be used to help meet the world's most pressing spiritual and physical needs through Business as Mission.[1]

---

1. See http://matstunehag.com/wp-content/uploads/2011/04/BAM-MANI FESTO-2.pdf.

CHAPTER 22

PRAY THROUGH YOUR BUSINESS WITH SAINT PATRICK

By Mats Tunehag

Every year on March 17, many people around the globe celebrate Saint Patrick—a human trafficking victim in the fifth century who became a missionary to the people and land (Ireland) where he once was enslaved.

Let me share a well-known prayer by Saint Patrick, and customize it to a BAM-related prayer (the original is in italics).[1] God cares for you and your business. Make him the center of it!

Christ with me, as I do business for him and people.

Christ before me, as I plan my business.

Christ behind me, as I review my business.

Christ in me, my guiding light in business.

Christ beneath me; he is the foundation.

Christ above me; he is the owner of my business

Christ on my right, Christ on my left; he is the Lord of the marketplace.

Christ when I lie down, and rest from my work.

Christ when I sit down, in my office chair.

---

1. Also available in Bahasa and Portuguese at http://matstunehag.com/2017/03/17/st-patricks-bam-prayer/.

Christ when I arise, enthusiastic or weary.

Christ in the heart of every man who thinks of me, and my business.

Christ in the mouth of everyone who speaks of me, and my business.

Christ in every eye that sees me, my staff, customers, suppliers, and competitors.

Christ in every ear that hears me speak about my products and services.

APPENDICES

WEALTH CREATION MANIFESTO

Lausanne Movement
Connecting influencers and ideas for global mission

BUSINESS AS MISSION
BAM GL●BAL

Background

The Lausanne Movement and BAM Global organized a Global Consultation on *The Role of Wealth Creation for Holistic Transformation*, in Chiang Mai, Thailand, in March 2017. About 30 people from 20 nations participated, primarily from the business world, and also from church, missions and academia. The findings will be published in several papers and a book, as well as an educational video. This Manifesto conveys the essentials of our deliberations before and during the Consultation.

Affirmations

1. Wealth creation is rooted in God the Creator, who created a world that flourishes with abundance and diversity.

2. We are created in God's image, to co-create with Him and for Him, to create products and services for the common good.

3. Wealth creation is a holy calling, and a God-given gift, which is commended in the Bible.

4. Wealth creators should be affirmed by the Church, and equipped and deployed to serve in the marketplace among all peoples and nations.

5. Wealth hoarding is wrong, and wealth sharing should be encouraged, but there is no wealth to be shared unless it has been created.

6. There is a universal call to generosity, and contentment is a virtue, but material simplicity is a personal choice, and involuntary poverty should be alleviated.

7. The purpose of wealth creation through business goes beyond giving generously, although that is to be commended; good business has intrinsic value as a means of material provision and can be an agent of positive transformation in society.

8. Business has a special capacity to create financial wealth, but also has the potential to create different kinds of wealth for many stakeholders, including social, intellectual, physical and spiritual wealth.

9. Wealth creation through business has proven power to lift people and nations out of poverty.

10. Wealth creation must always be pursued with justice and a concern for the poor, and should be sensitive to each unique cultural context.

11. Creation care is not optional. Stewardship of creation and business solutions to environmental challenges should be an integral part of wealth creation through business.

Appeal

We present these affirmations to the church worldwide, and especially to leaders in business, church, government, and academia.

- We call the church to embrace wealth creation as central to our mission of holistic transformation of peoples and societies.
- We call for fresh, ongoing efforts to equip and launch wealth creators to that very end.
- We call wealth creators to perseverance, diligently using their God-given gifts to serve God and people.

Ad maiorem Dei gloriam
For the greater glory of God

APPENDIX 2

CONSULTATION ON WEALTH CREATION

Background and Context

Held in March 2017 in Thailand, the Consultation on Wealth Creation (CWC) was part of broader, longer, ongoing conversations related to issues such as the church, business, poverty, wealth creation, and missions.

The CWC is another outcome of the historic commitments adopted in the Lausanne Covenant of 1974. Here, while committing themselves to the importance of evangelism, evangelicals also expressed repentance for "having sometimes regarded evangelism and social concern as mutually exclusive." Wealth creation for the economic betterment of our world is one of those neglected social concerns; and it is this that the CWC addresses.

At the 2017 consultation, all participants received a list of required reading related to their assignment of exploring the "Role of Wealth Creation in Holistic Transformation of People and Societies." Since the CWC was partly a follow-up of the Lausanne Global Consultation on Prosperity Theology, Poverty, and the Gospel (held in April 2014), participants needed to be familiar with the Atibaia Statement. Likewise, since the Wealth Creation Consultation collaborated with BAM Global (2004), some of its work and reports were included in the required reading.[1]

---

1. Required reading for the consultation included "Why Bother with Business as Mission?" by Mats Tunehag (http://matstunehag.com/wp-content/uploads /2011/04/Why-Bother-with-Business-as-Mission-v-18-April-2017.pdf); and the executive summaries of three BAM Global Think Tank reports: "Biblical Foundations for Business as Mission" (http://bamglobal.org/report-biblical), "Business as

In order to grasp the background and context of the seven CWC papers, it is important to understand some of the previous consultations which dealt with similar issues: the Lausanne BAM Issue Group (2004), the Wheaton Consultation (2009), and the Atibaia Consultation (2014).

The Lausanne BAM Issue Group

The first BAM Global Think Tank was held under the auspices of Lausanne. The Business as Mission Issue Group worked for a year, addressing issues relating to God's purposes for work and business, the role of businesspeople in church and missions, the needs of the world, and the potential response of business. It summarized its findings in the BAM Manifesto (2004). Here are a few excerpts to illustrate a growing consensus among leaders that wealth creators are called by God to serve in business.

- We believe that God *has created all men and women in his image with the ability to be creative, creating good things for themselves and for others—this includes business.*

- We believe in following in the footsteps of Jesus, who constantly and consistently met the needs of the people he encountered, thus demonstrating the love of God and the rule of his kingdom.

- We believe that the Holy Spirit *empowers all members of the* body of Christ *to serve and to meet the real spiritual and physical needs of others, demonstrating the kingdom of God.*

- We believe that God has called and equipped businesspeople to make a kingdom *difference in and through their businesses.*

- We believe that the gospel has the power to transform individuals, communities, and societies. Christians in business should therefore be a part of this holistic transformation through business.

Mission and the End of Poverty" (http://bamglobal.org/report-bop/), and "Business as Mission in Haiti" (http://bamglobal.org/report-haiti).

- We recognize the fact that poverty and unemployment are often rampant in areas where the name of Jesus is rarely heard and understood.

- We recognize that there is a need for job creation and for multiplication of businesses all over the world, aiming at the quadruple bottom line of spiritual, economic, social, and environmental transformation.

- We recognize the fact that the church has a huge and largely untapped resource in the Christian business community to meet the needs of the world—in and through business—bringing glory to God in the marketplace and beyond.[2]

Wheaton Consultation

In October 2009, a global consultation on "Business as Integral Calling" was held in Wheaton, Illinois. It brought theologians and academic leaders in business, economics, and missions together with leaders from business, nonprofit organizations, and Christian ministries. Excerpts from the declaration follow below.

Lamentations
- We lament that the church and business itself have undervalued business as a vehicle for living out Christ's calling, and have relied excessively on nonprofit approaches that have resulted in dependence, waste, and an unnecessary loss of human dignity.

Celebration of Faith and Hope
- We celebrate the growing movement of people seeking to be used by God to deploy business economic activity for God's kingdom.

- Business can create value, provide the dignity of work, and transform communities by improving livelihoods.

---

2. See also the BAM Manifesto (http://matstunehag.com/wp-ontent/uploads /2011/04/BAM-MANIFESTO-2.pdf).

- Business can be an integral calling to proclaim and demonstrate the kingdom of God by honoring God, loving people, and serving the world.

- Business can also provide a powerful opportunity for the transformation of individuals to achieve their full potential for creativity and productivity and to flourish and experience a life of abundance as envisioned in the kingdom of God.

- Business can be used to help restore God's creation from its degraded state.

- It is our deep conviction that businesses that function in alignment with the core values of the kingdom of God are playing and should increasingly play an important role in the holistic transformation of individuals, communities, and societies.[3]

Atibaia Consultation

Wealth creation and distribution were discussed as part of the Lausanne Global Consultation on Prosperity Theology, Poverty, and the Gospel held in Atibaia, Brazil, in 2014. The consultation affirmed that although sharing wealth is good and biblical, wealth distribution is too often our main response to meeting peoples' needs. This consultation identified the need to increasingly understand how businesses can bring solutions to global issues, including poverty and human trafficking. The notion of simplicity as a universal value was also challenged and needed to be addressed further.

Since the Atibaia Statement (https://www.lausanne.org/content/statement/atibaia-statement) is quite long, here are a few excerpts related to wealth creation, business, and the poor:

- Christians are called not only to give and share generously, but to work for the alleviation of poverty. This should include offering alternative, ethical ways for the creation of wealth and the maintenance of socially responsible businesses that empower the poor and provide material benefit and indi-

---

3. See also the Wheaton Declaration (http://matstunehag.com/wp-content/uploads/2017/05/Wheaton-Declaration.pdf).

vidual and communal dignity. This must always be done with the understanding that all wealth and all creation belong first and foremost to God.

- We acknowledge that, in the global market economy, one of the most effective tools for the elimination of poverty is economic development, yet evangelicals have often failed to promote value-driven business solutions to poverty.

- How can we more effectively work for the establishment of creative, ethical, and sustainable business endeavors in the fight against poverty?

Bibliography

Business as Mission & Economy: Books, Articles, and Papers

Adams, Bridget, and Manoj Raithatha. *Building the Kingdom through Business*. Watford: Instant Apostle, 2012.

Anonymous. "Business as Mission: The Effective Use of Tentmaking in North Africa." PhD diss., Southern Baptist Theological Seminary, 2011.

Baer, Michael. *2IC: Business as Mission for the Rest of Us*. N.p.: Amazon Digital, 2015. Kindle edition.

———. *Business as Mission: The Power of Business in the Kingdom of God*. Seattle, WA: YWAM Publishing, 2006.

———. *Gospel Entrepreneur: Starting a Kingdom Business*. N.p.: Amazon Digital, 2015. Kindle edition.

Bailey, Stephen. "Is Business as Mission Honest?" *Evangelical Missions Quarterly* 42:3 (2007): 368–72.

Baker, Dwogjt. "Missional Geometry: Plotting the Coordinates of Business as Mission." In *Business as Mission: From Impoverished to Empowered*, edited by Tom Steffen and Mike Barnett, 37–64. Pasadena, CA: William Carey Library, 2006.

Barrera, Albino. *Market Complicity and Christian Ethics*. Cambridge: Cambridge University Press, 2011.

Bas (pseudonym). "BAM in the Arab World." *St. Francis Magazine* 8:1 (2012): 16–21. http://www.stfrancismagazine.info/ja/content/view/626/38/.

Bates, Michael J. "Why Business as Mission Entrepreneurs Decided to Go into Business." *Business Journal for Entrepreneurs* 1 (2015): 78–106.

Befus, David. *Kingdom Business: The Ministry of Promoting Economic Development*. Miami: Latin America Mission, 2002.

———. "Kingdom Business Revisited: The Case of Northern Colombia." *Evangelical Missions Quarterly* 45:2 (2010): 158–64.

———. *Where There are No Jobs: Enterprise Solutions for Employment and Public Goods for the Poor*. Miami: Latin America Mission, 2005.

Bradley, Ian. *Enlightened Entrepreneurs: Business Ethics in Victorian Britain*. Oxford: Lion Hudson, 2007.

Bronkema, David, and Christopher Brown. "Business as Mission through the Lens of Development." *Transformation* 26:2 (2009): 82–88.

Bruni, Luigino, with Chiara Lubich. *The Economy of Communion: Toward a Multi-Dimensional Economic Culture*. New York: New City Press, 2002.

Christiansen, Linda. "Faith-based Social Entrepreneurship: Business as Mission." Masters thesis, Copenhagen Business School, Copenhagen, Denmark, 2008. http://studenttheses.cbs.dk/bit stream/handle/10417/681/linda_christiansen.pdf?sequence=1.

Corbett, Steve, and Brian Fikkert. *When Helping Hurts: How to Alleviate Poverty without Hurting the Poor . . . and Yourself*. Chicago: Moody Publishers, 2009.

Danker, William. *Profit for the Lord: Economic Activities in Moravian Missions and the Basel Mission Trading Company*. Eugene, OR: Wipf and Stock, 2002.

Dearborn, Tim. *Business as a Holy Calling? A Workbook for Christians in Business and Their Pastors*. N.p.: Createspace, 2014.

Eldred, Ken. *God Is at Work: Transforming People and Nations through Business*. Ventura, CA: Regal Books, 2005.

Erisman, Albert M. *The Accidental Executive: Lessons on Business, Faith and Calling from the Life of Joseph*. Peabody, MA: Hendrickson Publishers, 2015.

Ewert, Norm. "God's Kingdom Purpose for Business: Business as Integral Mission." In *Business as Mission: From Impoverished to Empowered*, edited by Tom Steffen and Mike Barnett, 19–36. Pasadena, CA: William Carey Library, 2006.

Gillespie, Teresa, and Timothy Lucas. "Blurring the Boundaries: Emerging Legal Forms for Hybrid Organizations, Implications for Christian Social Entrepreneurs." *The Journal of Biblical Integration in Business* 15:1 (2012): 11–28.

Goheem, William. *The Galtronics Story*. Eugene, OR: Wipf and Stock, 2004.

Gort, Gea, Mats Tunehag, and Monique Fahner. *Business as Mission; een wake-up call voor kerk, werk en samenleving*. Rotterdam: Gea Gort Urban Mission, 2015.

Grenz, Stanley. "God's Business: A Foundation for Christian Mission in the Marketplace." *Crux* 35:1 (1999): 19–25.

Griffiths, Brian, and Kim Tan. *Fighting Poverty through Enterprise: The Case for Social Venture Capital*. Ashford Kent: Anchor Recordings, 2007.

Grudem, Wayne. *Business for the Glory of God*. Wheaton, IL: Crossway, 2003.

Higginson, Richard. *Faith, Hope and the Global Economy: A Power for Good*. Downers Grove, IL: InterVarsity Press, 2012.

Interserve International. "Business as Mission: Best Practice Guidelines. *St. Francis Magazine* 8:1 (2012): 52–66. http://www.stfrancis magazine.info/ja/content/view/623/38/.

———. "Business as Mission: Task Force Report." *St. Francis Magazine* 8:1 (2012): 33–51. http://www.stfrancismagazine.info/ja/content/view/625/38/.

Jean-Louis, Daniel, and Jacqueline Klamer. *From Aid to Trade: How Aid Organizations, Businesses, and Governments Can Work Together: Lessons Learned from Haiti*. Ashland, OH: Fresh Strategy Press, 2016.

John Paul II. *Centesimus Annus*, 1991. http://w2.vatican.va/content/john-paul-ii/en/encyclicals/documents/hf_jp-ii_enc_0105 1991_centesimus-annus.html.

———. *Evangelium Vitae*, 1995. http://w2.vatican.va/content/john-paul-ii/en/encyclicals/documents/hf_jp-ii_enc_25031995 _evangelium-vitae.html.

———. *Veritas Splendor*, 1993. http://w2.vatican.va/content/john-paul-ii/en/encyclicals/documents/hf_jp-ii_enc_06081993_ver itatis-splendor.html.

Johnson, C. Neal. *Business as Mission: A Comprehensive Guide to Theory and Practice*. Downers Grove, IL: IVP Academic, 2009.

Johnson, C. Neal, and Steve Rundle. "The Distinctives and Challenges of Business as Mission." In *Business as Mission: From*

Impoverished to Empowered, edited by Tom Steffen and Mike Barnett, 19–36. Pasadena, CA: William Carey Library, 2006. http://businessasmission.com/wp-content/uploads/2014/04 /DistinctivesAndChallengesOfBusinessAsMission.pdf.

Kristof, Nicholas D., and Sheryl WuDunn. *A Path Appears: Transforming Lives, Creating Opportunity*. New York: Alfred A. Knopf, 2014.

Lai, Patrick. *Business for Transformation: Getting Started*. Pasadena, CA: William Carey Library, 2015.

———. "Problems and Solutions for Enhancing the Effectiveness of Tentmakers Doing Church Planting in the 10/40 Window." PhD diss., Asia Graduate School of Theology, Quezon City, Philippines, 2003.

———. "Starting a Business in a Restricted Access Nation." *International Journal of Frontier Missions* 15:1 (1998): 41–46.

———. *Tentmaking: Business as Mission*. Colorado Springs, CO: Authentic Media, 2005.

Lavoy, Deb. "Social Enterprise ROI: Measuring the Immeasurable" (2012). http://www.cmswire.com/cms/social-business/social -enterprise-roi-measuring-the-immeasurable-015149.php.

Leo XII. *Rerum Novarum*, 1891. http://w2.vatican.va/content/leo -xiii/en/encyclicals/documents/hf_l-xiii_enc_15051891_rerum -novarum.html.

Lingane, Alison, and Sara Olsen. "Guidelines for Social Return on Investment." *California Management Review* 46:3 (2004): 116–35.

Little, Christopher. "Business as Mission under Scrutiny." *Evangelical Missions Quarterly* 49:2 (2014): 177–85.

Little, Jerri. *Merchant to Romania: Business as Missions in Post-Communist Eastern Europe*. Leominster, UK: DayOne, 2009.

Livingstone, Greg. "Tentmaker's Credibility." *Evangelical Missions Quarterly* 30:1 (1994): 6.

Markiewicz, Mark. *Business as Mission: How Two Grocers Changed the Course of a Nation* (1999). http://www.intheworkplace.com /apps/articles/default.asp?articleid=12787&columnid=1935.

Miles, Toby. *7 Reasons Tentmaking Businesses Fail: Lessons Learned in Business as Mission*. N.p.: Amazon Digital, 2013. Kindle edition.

Miller, David. *God at Work: The History and Promise of the Faith at Work Movement*. New York: Oxford University Press, 2007.

Mills, Paul, and Michael Schluter. *After Capitalism: Rethinking Economic Relationships*. Cambridge: Jubilee Centre, 2012.

Mordomo, João. "Unleashing the Brazilian Missionary Force." In *Business as Mission: From Impoverished to Empowered*, edited by Tom Steffen and Mike Barnett, 219–39. Pasadena, CA: William Carey Library, 2006.

Moreau, A. Scott, and Mike O'Rear. "Business as Mission Resources." *Evangelical Missions Quarterly* 42:3 (2007): 380–86.

Moyo, Dambisa. *Dead Aid: Why Aid Is Not Working and How There Is Another Way for Africa*. London: Penguin Books, 2009.

Nichols, James. "Salience of Faith: The Role of Religious Values and Practices on Strategic Decision-Making of Christian Business Owners." PhD diss., Anderson University, Anderson, Indiana, 2010.

Nordstrom, Dwight, and Jim Nielsen. "How Business Is Integral to Tentmaking." *International Journal of Frontier Missions* 15:1 (1998): 15–18.

Norrish, Howard. "Lone Ranger: Yes or No?" *Evangelical Missions Quarterly* 26 (1990): 6–14.

Novak, Michael. *Business as a Calling: Work and the Examined Life*. New York: The Free Press, 1996.

Owens, Howard. "Nestorian Merchant Missionaries and Today's Unreached People Groups." In *Business as Mission: From Impoverished to Empowered*, edited by Tom Steffen and Mike Barnett, 133–46. Pasadena, CA: William Carey Library, 2006.

Packer, J. I. "The Christian's Purpose in Business." In *Biblical Principles and Business: The Practice*, edited by Richard C. Chewning, 16–25. Colorado Springs, CO: NavPress, 1990.

Pointer, Steven, and Michael Cooper. "Seventeenth-century Puritan Missions: Some Implications for Business as Mission." In *Business as Mission: From Impoverished to Empowered*, edited by Tom Steffen and Mike Barnett, 167–80. Pasadena, CA: William Carey Library, 2006.

Quattro, Scott A. (2012). "Is Business as Mission a Flawed Concept? A Reformed Christian Perspective on the BAM Movement." *The Journal of Biblical Integration in Business* 15:1 (2012): 80–87. http://www.cbfa.org/JBIBVol15No1.pdf.

Roche, Bruno, and Jay Jakub. *Completing Capitalism: Heal Business to Heal the World*. Oakland, CA: Berrett-Koehler, 2017.

Rotheroe, Neil, and Adam Richards. "Social Return on Investment and Social Enterprise: Transparent Accountability for Sustainable Development." *Social Enterprise Journal* 3:1 (2007): 31–48.

Rundle, Steve. "Business as Mission Hybrids: A Review and Research Agenda." *Journal of Biblical Integration in Business* 15:1 (2012): 66–79. http://www.cbfa.org/JBIBVol15No1.pdf.

———. "The Christian Business Scholar and the Great Commission: A Proposal for Expanding the Agenda." *Journal of Biblical Integration in Business* (2000): 94–108.

———. "Does Donor Support Help or Hinder BAM Practitioners? An Empirical Assessment." *International Bulletin of Missionary Research* 38:1 (2014): 21–26. http://www.internationalbulletin.org/system/files/2014-01-021-rundle.pdf.

———. "Ministry, Profits, and the Schizophrenic Tentmaker." *Evangelical Missions Quarterly* 36:3 (2000): 292–300.

———. "Preparing the Next Generation of Kingdom Entrepreneurs." In *On Kingdom Business: Transforming World Mission through Kingdom Entrepreneurs*, edited by Tetsunao Yamamori and Kenneth Eldred, 225–44. Wheaton, IL: Crossway Books, 2003.

———. "Restoring the Role of Business in Mission." In *Perspectives on the World Christian Movement*, edited by R. D. Winter and S. C. Hawthorne. 4th ed., 757–63. Pasadena, CA: William Carey Library, 2009.

Rundle, Steve, and Tom Steffen. *Great Commission Companies: The Emerging Role of Business in Missions*. Downers Grove, IL: InterVarsity Press, 2011.

Rundle, Steve, and Thomas Sudyk. "Funding a Kingdom Company." *Evangelical Missions Quarterly* 43:4 (2007): 442–48.

Russell, Mark. "The Biblical Basis for the Integration of Business and Missions." In *Business as Mission: From Impoverished to Empowered*, edited by Tom Steffen and Mike Barnett, 117–31. Pasadena, CA: William Carey Library, 2006.

———. *The Missional Entrepreneur: Principles and Practices for Business as Mission*. Birmingham, AL: New Hope, 2010.

———. "The Use of Business in Missions in Chiang Mai, Thailand." PhD diss., Asbury Theological Seminary, Wilmore, Kentucky, 2008.

Schumacher, Heinrich Vollrat, and Marco Gmür. *Business Power for God's Purpose*. Greng, Switzerland: VKG Publishing, 1997.

Sedlacek, Tomas. *Economics of Good and Evil: The Quest for Economic Meaning from Gilgamesh to Wall Street*. New York: Oxford University Press, 2011.

Seebeck, Doug, and Timothy Stoner. *My Business, My Mission*. Grand Rapids: Partners Worldwide, 2009.

Silvoso, Ed. *Anointed for Business: How to Use Your Influence in the Marketplace to Change the World*. Ventura, CA: Regal Books, 2002.

Steffen, Tom, and Mike Barnett, eds. *Business as Mission: From Impoverished to Empowered*. Pasadena, CA: William Carey Library, 2006.

Swarr, Sharon Bentch, and Dwight Nordstrom. *Transform the World: Biblical Vision and Purpose for Business*. Center for Entrepreneurship and Economic Development, 1999.

Tongoi, Dennis. "The Challenges and Opportunities for Business as Mission: A Perspective from Africa." *Connections* 8:2 (2009): 1–3.

Tunehag, Mats. *"Business as Mission"* (2001). http://www.globalcon nections.co.uk/pdfs/businessasmissiontunehag.pdf.

———. *"A Global Overview of the Business as Mission Movement: Needs and Gaps"* (2008). http://www.lausanne.org/all-docu ments/needs-gaps.html.

———. *"God Means Business!"* (2008). http://www.matstunehag. com/wp-content/uploads/2011/04/God-Means-Business2.pdf.

———. *"The Mission of Business: CSR+"* (2009). http://www.mats tunehag.com/wp-content/uploads/2011/04/The-Mission-of -Business-CSR+1.pdf.

———. *"Why Bother with Business as Mission?"* (2017). http://mats tunehag.com/wp-content/uploads/2011/04/Why-Bother-with -Business-as-Mission-v-18-April-2017.pdf

Tunehag, Mats, Wayne McGee, and Jo Plummer. "Business as Mission." *The Lausanne Occasional Paper*, no. 59 (2004). http:// www.lausanne.org/documents/2004forum/LOP59_IG30.pdf.

Tunehag, Mats, and Peter Shaukat. "Business." In *Global Dictionary of Theology*, edited by William Dyrness and Veli-Matti Kärk-käinen, 125–26. Downers Grove, IL: InterVarsity Press, 2008. http://www.matstunehag.com/wp-content/uploads/2011/04 /IVP-article-0806.pdf.

———. *"Why Is Bangladesh Poor and Taiwan Rich?"* (2009). http://www. matstunehag.com/wp-content/uploads/2011/04/WEA-MC -Paper-on-Why-is-Bangladesh-poor-and-Taiwan-rich-May -091.pdf.

Tunehag, Mats, and Jennifer Tunehag. *"Business Solutions to Human Trafficking"* (2016). http://matstunehag.com/wp-content/up loads/2011/04/CEF-2016-biz-solution-to-tip.pdf.

Turnbull, Richard. *Quaker Capitalism: Lessons for Today.* Oxford: Centre for Enterprise, Markets and Ethics, 2016.

Van Duzer, Jeff. *Why Business Matters to God (And What Still Needs to Be Fixed).* Downers Grove, IL: IVP Academic, 2010.

Yamamori, Tetsunao. *God's New Envoys: A Bold Strategy for Penetrating Closed Countries.* Portland, OR: Multnomah Press, 1987.

———. *Penetrating Missions' Final Frontier: A New Strategy for Unreached Peoples.* Downers Grove, IL: InterVarsity Press, 1993.

Yamamori, Tetsunao, and Kenneth Eldred, eds. *On Kingdom Business: Transforming Mission through Entrepreneurial Strategies.* Wheaton, IL: Crossway Books, 2003.

Other BAM Resources

For an extensive list of books about Business as Mission:

- businessasmission.com/library/books
- businessasmission.com/library/bibliography

BAM material available in nineteen languages:

- matstunehag.com/bam-material-in-different-languages

BAM Think Tank Reports:

- matstunehag.com/bam-think-tank-reports

Recommended websites about Business as Mission:

- businessasmission.com
- matstunehag.com
- bamglobal.org

Videos about Business as Mission:

- matstunehag.com/videos

Seven papers on Wealth Creation:

- bamglobal.org/reports

Wealth Creation Manifesto in more than a dozen languages:

- matstunehag.com/wealth-creation

Universities, Business Schools, Mission Organizations, and Churches

There are a growing number of universities and colleges around the world that are teaching BAM, have BAM programs, or have made BAM the very DNA of their curriculum. Similarly, most of the oldest and largest mission organizations in the world have embraced BAM. There are also a growing number of churches and denominations doing the same. For regular updates on BAM, sign up for the biweekly *BAM Review* at www.businessasmission.com.

Theology of Work

Bakke, Dennis, W. *Joy at Work: A Revolutionary Approach to Fun on the Job*. Seattle: PVG, 2005.

Bakke, Raymond, William Hendricks, and Brad Smith. *Joy at Work: Bible Study Companion*. Seattle: PVG, 2005.

Block, Peter. *Stewardship: Choosing Service over Self-Interest*. San Francisco: Berret-Koehler, 1993.

Cosden, Darrell. *The Heavenly Good of Earthly Work*. Peabody, MA: Hendrickson Publishers / UK: Paternoster Press, 2006.

Dijk, Joost van. *Sowing the New Creation. The Purpose of Work and Business from the Perspective of the New Creation*. The Netherlands, 2014. https://sowingthenewcreation.wordpress.com.

Greenleaf, Robert K. *Servant Leadership: A Journey into the Nature of Legitimate Power and Greatness*. New York: Paulist Press, 1977.

Messenger, Will, ed. *Theology of Work Bible Commentary*. Peabody, MA: Hendrickson Publishers, 2016.

Stevens, Paul R. *Doing God's Business: Meaning and Motivation for the Marketplace*. Grand Rapids: Eerdmans, 2006.

———. *The Other Six Days: Vocation, Work, and Ministry in Biblical Perspective*. Grand Rapids: Eerdmans, 1999.

Stevens, Paul R., and Robert Banks, eds. *The Marketplace Ministry Handbook*. Vancouver, BC: Regent College, 2005.

Volf, Miroslav. *Work in the Spirit: Toward a Theology of Work*. Eugene, OR: Wipf and Stock, 2001.

Community/Urban Transformation

Bakke, Ray. *A Theology as Big as the City*. Downers Grove, IL: InterVarsity Press, 1997.

Batstone, David. *Not for Sale: The Return of the Global Slave Trade—and How We Can Fight It*. New York: Harper Collins, 2010.

Block, Peter. *Community: The Structure of Belonging*. San Francisco: Berrett-Koehler, 2009.

Conn, Harvie M., and Manuel Ortiz. *Urban Ministry*. Downers Grove, IL: InterVarsity Press, 2001.

Gort, Gea. *God in the City: A Missional Way of Life in an Urban Context*. Seattle: Harmon Digital Press, 2012.

Halter, Hugh, and Matt Smay. *The Tangible Kingdom*. San Francisco: Jossey-Bass, 2008.

Hayes, John B. *Sub–Merge: Living Deep in a Shallow World*. Ventura, CA: Regal Books, 2006.

Linthicum, Robert. *Transforming Power: Biblical Strategies for Making a Difference in Your Community*. Downers Grove, IL: InterVarsity Press, 2003.

Lupton, Robert D. *Renewing the City: Reflections on Community Development and Urban Renewal*. Downers Grove, IL: InterVarsity Press, 2005.

Neilson, Peter. *Church on the Move: New Church, New Generation, New Scotland*. Glasgow: Covenanters, 2005.

Sparks, Paul, Tim Soerens, and Dwight J. Friesen. *The New Parish: How Neighborhood Churches are Transforming Mission, Discipleship, and Community*. Downers Grove, IL: InterVarsity Press, 2014.

Stark, Rodney. *Cities of God: The Real Story of How Christianity Became an Urban Movement and Conquered Rome*. New York: Harper Collins, 2006.

White, Randy. *Encounter God in the City: Onramps to Personal and Community Transformation*. Downers Grove, IL: InterVarsity Press, 2006.

———. "The Work of Our Hands: Faith Rooted Approaches to Job Creation, Training or Placement in a Context of Concentrated Poverty" (2012). http://www.condeopress.com.

Woodberry, Robert D. "The Missionary Roots of Liberal Democracy." *American Political Science Review* 106, no. 2 (May 2012).

Other Resources Related to Gea Gort's Chapters

Bakke, Ray. *Global Church History*. DVD series. Wheaton, IL: Wheaton College, 1988.

Bartholomew, Craig G., and Michael W. Goheen. *The Drama of Scripture*. Grand Rapids: Baker Academic, 2007.

Bloom, Anthony. *School for Prayer*. London: Libra Books / Darton, Longman & Todd, 1970.

Bria, Ion. *Liturgy after the Liturgy: Mission and Witness from an Orthodox Perspective*. Switzerland: World Council of Churches, 1996.

Brueggemann, Walter. *An Introduction to the Old Testament*. Louisville: Westminster John Knox Press, 2003.

Fee, Gordon D., and Douglas Stuart. *How to Read the Bible for All It's Worth*. Grand Rapids: Zondervan, 2003.

Gent, Rien van. "Foundations and Society: Sliding Panels." Lecture, European Cultural Foundation, 2016. http://www.culturalfoundation.eu/library/foundations-and-society-sliding-panels-rien-van-gendt-lecture.

Goheen, Michael W. "The Urgency of Reading the Bible as One Story in the Twenty-first Century." Public lecture given at Regent College, Vancouver, BC, November 2, 2006.

Gonzalez, Justo L. *The Story of Christianity: The Early Church to the Dawn of the Reformation*. Vol. 1. San Francisco: Harper and Row, 1984.

———. *The Story of Christianity: The Reformation to the Present Day*. Vol. 2. San Francisco: Harper and Row, 1985.

Griffin, Winn. *God's Epic Adventure*. Woodinville, WA: Harmon Press, 2007.

Nassif, Bradley, Michael Horton, Vladimir Berzonsky, George Hancock Stefan, and Edward Rommen. *Counterpoints: Three Views on Eastern Orthodox Evangelicalism*. Grand Rapids: Zondervan, 2004.

Oleksa, Michael. *Orthodox Alaska: A Theology of Mission*. New York: St. Vladimir's Seminary Press, 1992.

Raschke, Carl. *GloboChrist: The Great Commission Takes a Postmodern Turn*. Grand Rapids: Baker Academic, 2008.

Schluter, Michael, and David John Lee. *The R Option: Building Relationships as a Better Way of Life*. Cambridge: The Relationships Foundation, 2003.

Tickle, Phyllis. *The Great Emergence*. Grand Rapids: Baker Books, 2008.

Ware, Kallistos. *The Orthodox Way*. Rev. ed. New York: St. Vladimir's Seminary Press, 1995.

Wright, Christopher. *The Mission of God*. Nottingham, UK: InterVarsity Press, 2006.

Wright, N. T. *The Challenge of Jesus*. Downers Grove, IL: InterVarsity Press, 1999.

———. *How Can The Bible Be Authoritative?* The Laing Lecture 1989 and the Griffith Thomas Lecture 1989. Originally published in *Vox Evangelica* (1991), http://www.ntwrightpage.com/Wright_Bible_Authoritative.htm.

———. *Surprised by Hope: Rethinking Heaven, the Resurrection, and the Mission of the Church*. New York: HarperCollins, 2007.

Author Biographies

Dr. Gea Gort (www.GeaGort.com), a trained journalist, studied transformational leadership in the global urban context at Bakke Graduate University in Dallas, Texas, where she serves as adjunct faculty and is a regional board member. She is passionate about innovative mission in an urban and global context. In her hometown of Rotterdam (Holland), she initiated City Prayer, directed a Christian leader's network, and advised the government on multicultural affairs. With her husband, she served onboard Mercy Ships' hospital ships and started Mercy Ships Holland. Gea has authored several books in Dutch and in English.

Mats Tunehag (www.MatsTunehag.com) is a speaker, writer, and consultant from Sweden and has worked in more than half the countries of the world. He has been a global thought leader for the Business as Mission (BAM) movement for over twenty years. Tunehag is the chairman of BAM Global and has led two global BAM think tanks. Tunehag has served as a senior leader in BAM for both the Lausanne Movement and World Evangelical Alliance, and was the convener of the Global Consultation on the Role of Wealth Creation for Holistic Transformation. Tunehag serves part time with a global investment fund that helps SMEs to grow in size and holistic impact in the Arab world and Asia.

ABOUT THE HENDRICKSON PUBLISHERS/ THEOLOGY OF WORK LINE OF BOOKS

There is an unprecedented interest today in the role of Christian faith in "ordinary" work, and Christians in every field are exploring what it means to work "as to the Lord" (Col. 3:22). Pastors and church leaders, and the scholars and teachers who support them, are asking what churches can do to equip their members in the workplace. There's a need for deep thinking, fresh perspectives, practical ideas, and mutual engagement between Christian faith and work in every sphere of human endeavor.

This Hendrickson Publishers/Theology of Work line of books seeks to bring significant new resources into this conversation. It began with Hendrickson's publication of the *Theology of Work Bible Commentary* and other Bible study materials written by the TOW Project. Soon we discovered a wealth of resources by other writers with a common heart for the meaning and value of everyday work. The HP/TOW line was formed to make the best of these resources available on the national and international stage.

Works in the HP/TOW line engage the practical issues of daily work through the lens of the Bible and the other resources of the Christian faith. They are biblically grounded, but their subjects are the work, workers, and workplaces of today. They employ contemporary arts and sciences, best practices, empirical research, and wisdom gained from experience, yet always in the service of Christ's redemptive work in the world, especially the world of work.

To a greater or lesser degree, all the books in this line make use of the scholarship of the *Theology of Work Bible Commentary*. The authors, however, are not limited to the TOW Project's perspectives, and they constantly expand the scope and application of the material. Publication of a book in the HP/TOW line does not necessarily imply endorsement by the Theology of Work Project, or that the author endorses the TOW Project. It does mean we recognize the work as an important contribution to the faith-work discussion, and we find a common footing that makes us glad to walk side-by-side in the dialogue.

We are proud to present the HP/TOW line together. We hope it helps readers expand their thinking, explore ideas worthy of deeper thought, and make sense of their own work in light of the Christian faith. We are grateful to the authors and all those whose labor has brought the HP/TOW line to life.

William Messenger, Executive Editor, Theology of Work Project
Sean McDonough, Biblical Editor, Theology of Work Project
Patricia Anders, Editorial Director, Hendrickson Publishers

www.theologyofwork.org
www.hendrickson.com